GOD

IS

A PERSON

GOD

IS

A PERSON

Reflections of Two
NOBEL LAUREATES

Open dialogues with

Dr. T. D. Singh
(H. H. Bhaktisvarupa Damodara Swami)

Bhaktivedanta Institute
Kolkata

Published by
The Bhaktivedanta Institute
RC/8, Raghunathpur
Manasi Manjil Building, Fourth Floor
VIP Road, Kolkata - 700 059
www.binstitute.org

Editor: T. D. Singh, Ph. D.

Cover Design: Jivanmukta Das, Sacirani Devi Dasi and Vrajapati Das

Illustrations: Vrajapati Das

Printed by
Anderson Printing House Pvt. Ltd., Kolkata

ISBN: 81-89635-03-4

Dedicated to

His Divine Grace
A. C. Bhaktivedanta Swami Srila Prabhupada
(1896–1977)
A Visionary Saint for the Modern Scientific Age
& Founder Acharya of The Bhaktivedanta Institute

ACKNOWLEDGMENTS

We sincerely acknowledge the research and editorial assistance rendered by Dr. Sudipto Ghosh, Phalguni Banerjee, Varun Agarwal, and K. Vasudeva Rao. Further, we would like to thank Sriman Jivanmukta Das, Srimati Sacirani Devi Dasi and Sriman Vrajapati Das for providing the illustrations and the cover design for the book. We also heartily acknowledge the dedicated services of Sri Arun Uday, Sriman Saunak Muni Das, Sriman Padmalochan Das, Sriman Abhijit Das and Sriman Dina Anukampana Das in the production of this volume. The publication of this book is partly funded by the Metanexus Institute, Philadelphia, USA, under its Local Societies Initiative (LSI) program. We gratefully acknowledge the financial support and encouragement given by the Metanexus Institute to the Bhaktivedanta Institute's Science and Religion Group of Kolkata.

CONTENTS

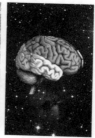

Perceiving God

Quotes on God by Some Prominent Scientists

Nicholas Copernicus
(1473-1543)

$\mathcal{T}$he universe has been brought for us by a supremely good and orderly Creator.

— Nicholas Copernicus

Johannes Kepler
(1571-1630)

I have endeavored to gain for human reason, aided by geometrical calculation, an insight into His way of creation; may the Creator of the heavens themselves, the father of all reason, to whom our mortal senses owe their existence, may He who is Himself immortal . . . keep me in His grace and guard me from reporting anything about His work which cannot be justified before His magnificence or which may misguide our powers of reason, and may He cause us to aspire to the perfection of His works of creation by the dedication of our lives. . . ."

— Johannes Kepler

Isaac Newton
(1642-1727)

*T*his most beautiful system of the sun,
planet and comets, could only proceed from
the counsel and dominion of an intelligent and
powerful Being.

— Isaac Newton

Michael Faraday
(1791-1867)

*W*e ought to value the privilege of knowing God's truth far beyond anything we can have in this world.

— Michael Faraday

James Clerk Maxwell
(1831-1879)

*A*lmighty God, Who has created man in Thine own image, and made him a living soul that he might seek after Thee, and have dominion over Thy creatures, teach us to study the works of Thy hands, that we may subdue the earth to our use, and strengthen the reason for Thy service; so to receive Thy blessed Word, that we may believe on Him Who Thou has sent, to give us the knowledge of salvation and the remission of our sins.

— James Clerk Maxwell

Albert Einstein
(1879-1955)

$\mathcal{M}$y religion consists of a humble admiration for this illimitable superior spirit that reveals itself in the slight details that we are able to perceive with our frail and feeble minds. That deeply emotional conviction of the presence of a superior reasoning power which is revealed in the comprehensible universe forms my idea of God.

— Albert Einstein

Max Born
(1882-1970)

I saw in it (the atom) the key to the deepest secret of nature, and it revealed to me the greatness of the creation and the Creator.

— Max Born

Srinivasa A. Ramanujan
(1887-1920)

*A*n equation for me has no meaning,
unless it represents a thought of God.

— Srinivasa A. Ramanujan

Werner Heisenberg
(1901-1976)

$\mathcal{T}$here is a higher power, not influenced by our wishes, which finally decides and judges.

— Werner Heisenberg

Introduction

T. D. Singh

*International Director,
Bhaktivedanta Institute
& President, Vedanta
and Science Educational
Research Foundation*

The nature of the human soul is to explore the underlying secrets of the visible as well as the invisible worlds, to investigate the unknown and finally to inquire about the nature of the Ultimate Reality or God. The mind, the senses and the intelligence are instruments in this dynamic and most worthwhile exercise. Scientific knowledge is born out of such inquiry. Religious knowledge or spiritual wisdom is also aimed at finding and realizing the same Ultimate Reality.

According to the Vedanta, there are four defects of the senses. They are: (i) *Bhrama* (illusion), for example, a mirage seen in the desert; (ii) *Pramāda* (mistake), for example, a rope maybe mistaken for a snake; (iii) *Karaṇāpāṭava* (limitation), for example, we cannot hear sounds below 20 Hz (infrasonic) and above 20,000 Hz (ultrasonic); and (iv) *Vipralipsā* (cheat), for example, when the senses are overcome by pride, false ego, lusty desire and arrogance, one's propensity to cheat becomes predominant. Thus scientific knowledge, which is gathered by sense perception is very limited and we can grasp only a small fraction of reality. Scientific knowledge, therefore, cannot prove the existence of God. In other words, *āroha-panthā*, or the bottom-up approach is not sufficient to gain substantial knowledge of God. The timeless message of the Vedas proclaim that God can be understood through revealed knowledge, scriptures. Vedanta describes *sāstrayonitvat* – scriptures can give knowledge of God. This is called the *avaroha-panthā*, the top-down or *parampara* process.

The ancient Vedic scripture known as *Śrīmad-Bhāgavatam* or *Bhāgavata Purāṇa*, the most ripened fruit of the Vedic tree of knowledge describes the three aspects of God realization as follows:

> *vadanti tat tattva-vidas*
> *tattvaṁ yaj jñānam advayam*
> *brahmeti paramātmeti*
> *bhagavān iti śabdyate*

Translation: Learned transcendentalists who know the Absolute Truth call this non-dual substance *Brahman* (the attributeless Absolute), *Paramātmā* (the indwelling Supersoul), or *Bhagavān* (the Supreme Lord Himself).[1]

Brahman or the impersonal aspect of God realization is achieved by the students of the Upanishads, the philosophical literatures of the Vedas. It is an incomplete realization of God. Similarly, many scientists such as Einstein could grasp the impersonal aspect of God to some degree by their own experience of scientific investigation. Einstein was greatly impressed by observing the order and beauty of the laws of nature, grandeur and the mystical aspects of the universe. He remarked, "I believe in mystery and, frankly, I sometimes face this mystery with great fear. In other words, I think there are many things in the universe that we cannot perceive or penetrate and that also we experience some of the most beautiful things in life in only a very primitive form. Only in relation to these mysteries do I consider myself to be a religious man. But I sense these things deeply… the most beautiful and most profound religious emotion that we can experience is the sensation of the mystical. And this mysticality is the power of all true science… In essence, my religion consists of a humble admiration for this illimitable superior spirit that reveals itself in the slight details that we are able to perceive with our frail and feeble minds. That deeply emotional conviction of the presence of a superior reasoning power which is revealed in the comprehensible universe forms my idea of God."[2]

Paramātmā realization is achieved by the *yogīs*. *Paramātmā* is an indwelling partial expansion of the personality aspect of God, localized in all living entities primarily for guiding them in every aspect. It is the *Paramātmā* from within that guides, inspires and gives creativity to the individual in scientific discoveries, musical composition and fine artistic works. However, according to Vedic scriptures, the *Brahman* and the *Paramātmā* realization is a partial understanding of God.

Realization of *Bhagavān* is the realization of the supreme personality aspect of God and this is realized by sincere devotees and servants of God. According to the Vedas, this is the highest aspect of God realization.

According to Vedanta, God has three kinds of internal potency or energy, namely, the (i) *Sandhinī-śakti*, or existential potency, (ii) *Saṁvit-śakti*, or cognitive potency and the (iii) *Hlādinī-śakti* or pleasure potency. This is also confirmed in the *Viṣṇu Purāṇa* (1.12.69). In the *Bhāgavata-sandarbha* (103), Srila Jiva Goswami explains these transcendental attributes of God elaborately (CC Adi 4.60).[3] The living beings are also endowed with these attributes in different degrees.

The Absolute Truth, God is the transcendental Reality (*cit-svarūpa*) possessing all these attributes in full. The manifestation of these internal potencies or energies of the Lord is the inconceivable variegated spiritual world (*cit-jagat*), the manifestation of the marginal energy of the Lord comprises the living entities, and the manifestation of the external energy of the Lord is the material cosmos (CC Adi 4.62 purport).

Thus God, the Absolute Truth includes these four principles – the Supreme Godhead Himself, His internal energy, His marginal energy and His external energy.

The form of the Lord (*svayaṁ-rūpa*) and the expansions of His form (*vaibhava-prakāśa*) are directly enjoyers of the internal energy in the spiritual world. The external manifestation, the material energy, provides the material bodies of all the conditioned living entities manifesting as biodiversity.

In order to manifest the physical universe, God manifests Himself as three expansions called *puruṣa-avatāras*, namely Mahā-Viṣṇu, Garbhodakaśāyī Viṣṇu, and Kṣīrodakaśāyī Viṣṇu to fulfill the desires of every living being according to the karma of every being. Mahā-Viṣṇu is the source of all physical universes and Garbhodakaśāyī Viṣṇu enters in each universe and Kṣīrodakaśāyī Viṣṇu enters into each living being and atom as *paramātmā* and guides every living being from microorganisms to human beings to demigods. In this way the whole material world is run and maintained.[4]

Thus the cosmic creation and dissolution go on periodically according to the Big Vision of the Supreme Lord. The creation of this physical universe is the facility given to conditioned living beings by God in order to get liberated from the false conception of life (materialism).

According to ancient Vedic culture, religious principles are directly given by God to guide the human beings – *dharmaṁ tu sākṣād bhagavat-praṇītaṁ* (*Śrīmadbhāgavatam* 6.3.19). The essence of all religious teachings consists of morality, ethics, humility and love of God. Spiritual or religious life is an important aspect for every human being. It provides moral codes of living in order to get free from the bondage of worldly life and thus qualify to return to the spiritual world. All these will be achieved by developing the *sambandha-jñāna* - the knowledge of personal relationship of the individual being with God knowing that the living being is fully dependent on the mercy of Supreme Godhead as a conscious spiritual particle or spiriton of God. Thus the next step which is to adopt *abhidheya* – which culminates in unalloyed devotional service to the Supreme Lord – which consists of nine devotional activities (*nava-vidhā bhakti*) – (a) *śravaṇam* (hearing); (b) *kīrtanam* (chanting); (c) *Viṣṇoḥ smaraṇam* (remembering); (d) *pāda-sevanam* (serving the lotus feet); (e) *arcanam* (offering worship); (f) *vandanam* (offering prayers); (g) *dāsyam* (becoming the servant); (h) *sakhyam* (becoming the friend); (i) *ātma-nivedanam* (surrendering everything to the Lord) – which will lead to *prayojana* – attaining the highest goal of life, which is love of God. Further works in this connection will be presented elsewhere.

These different states of realization of God may be referred to as spiritual dynamics or states in the study of God. The first two aspects can be referred to as intermediary aspects whereas the third state is the final state in the study of the science of God, according to Vedanta. Besides, in the study of the science of life, various spiritual elements such as – nobility, compassion, humility, gentleness, love, respect, morality, etc., are all different aspects of spiritual dynamics. Many scientists and philosophers are attracted by the impersonal aspects of God. However, the vaisnava scientific and theological culture of India elaborately describes that in order to understand the personal aspect of God one has to learn *bhakti yoga,* a devotional science involving nine processes of spiritual dynamics (*nava-vidhā bhakti)* mentioned above.

We are pleased to present in this volume the thoughts, wisdom, sincere feelings and experiences of personal relationship with God of two great scientists of our time – Prof. Charles H. Townes and Prof. William D. Phillips. Both are Nobel Laureates in Physics. Charles Townes received the Nobel Prize in physics in 1964 for his discovery of laser and maser and William Phillips was awarded the 1997 Nobel Prize for his pioneering work of cooling and trapping neutral atoms using lasers. We hope these dialogues will help our readers to further shape their perceptions about the nature of the Ultimate Reality or God.

Notes and References

1. A.C. Bhaktivedanta Swami Śrīla Prabhupāda, *Śrīmadbhāgavatam*, Canto 1, Ch. 2 Verse 11, Bhaktivedanta Book Trust, Bombay, 1987, p.103.
2. Lincoln Barnett, *The Universe and Dr. Einstein*, 2nd Edition (Tenth Printing), New York, 1957, pp. 108-109.
3. CC Adi 4.60 refers to: A.C. Bhaktivedanta Swami Śrīla Prabhupāda, *Śrī Caitanya Caritāmṛta*, Ādi-Lilā 4.60, Bhaktivedanta Book Trust, Bombay, 1996.
4. *Savijñānam – Scientific Exploration for a Spiritual Paradigm*, Kolkata, 2003, vol.2, pp. 92-94.

IMPORTANCE OF SCIENCE-RELIGION DIALOGUE
AND
PERSONAL INTERACTION WITH GOD

LASERS

Lasers are so common now. We use them like pencils – from supermarket checkouts and CD players to laser surgery, laser printers and laser light shows. Thanks to Charles Townes for his amazing discovery of laser. An original thinker and prolific scientist, Townes is equally deep in spiritual dimensions of life. According to him God is very personal and there is continuous interaction between God and this universe, especially with us personally. It is extremely important for him.

$\mathscr{C}$harles Townes, the Nobel laureate whose inventions include the maser and laser, has spent decades as a leading advocate for the convergence of science and religion. Last year, he also won the 2005 Templeton Prize. Townes, who celebrated his 90th birthday last year, secured his place in the pantheon of great 20th-century scientists through his investigations into the properties of microwaves which resulted first in the maser, a device which amplifies electromagnetic waves, and later his co-invention of the laser, which amplifies and directs light waves into parallel direct beams. His research, for which he shared the Nobel Prize in Physics in 1964, opened the door for an astonishing array of inventions and discoveries now in common use throughout the world in medicine, telecommunications, electronics, computers, and other areas.

But for Townes, his discovery of the principles of the maser and the laser was an inspiration from God — "the inspiration came from God." The personal interaction with God is extremely important for him. God is not just some distant thing that created the universe and then left it alone. He says, "God is very personal. He has very personal interactions with us … I think there is continuous interaction between God and this universe, especially with us personally. That is very important to our lives."

Dr. T. D. Singh, International Director of the Bhaktivedanta Institute, Kolkata, visited him at his office at the University of California, Berkeley, USA. Dr. Singh is himself a scientist with a doctorate in physical organic chemistry from the University of California, Irvine and also a spiritualist of the Bhaktivedanta tradition of India. He studied Vedantic theology under Srila A. C. Bhaktivedanta Swami Prabhupada, the most well-known propounder of Vedic science and culture of the twentieth century throughout the world. He has been a pioneer in advancing dialogue between science and religion for over 30 years.

The following pages present a classic dialogue: "Importance of Science—Religion Dialogue and Personal Interaction with God" between Charles Townes and T. D. Singh. It took place at the University of California, Berkeley, USA on May 13, 2005.

കൃ

Charles **H Townes** (Henceforth **CHT**): Welcome Dr. Singh. It is very nice to see you again. So how are your efforts for promoting dialogue between science and spirituality progressing?

Dr. T.D. Singh (Henceforth **TDS**): Thank you Prof. Townes. I am trying my best. I am very impressed that in today's world, many scientists are increasingly participating in the discussions on science and spirituality. You yourself are contributing significantly in this area. I feel that it is important for our readers to hear from you and receive some of your scientific and religious wisdom.

CHT: All right.

TDS: First of all, I would like to say that besides being a great scientist you are well-known for appreciating religious and spiritual values in scientific works. When discussions of the various conceptions of God are brought out in science and religion dialogue, they are often unclear. Can you, as a scientist, say anything about the understanding of God?

CHT: You want to know how I, as a scientist, understand God?

TDS: Yes.

CHT: Well, understanding God is certainly very difficult. I would say there is some spiritual force out there that has planned this

universe and is affecting us, and I feel a very close personal interaction. It is very important to me.

TDS: What about the argument within scientific communities that the universe is fine-tuned? You yourself have mentioned that our universe is very special and unique. The fundamental constants, especially, are made in such a unique way; any slight change in these constants might lead to a completely different type of universe.[1] The universe as we know it would be completely different. I'd like to say that this type of interpretation could be taken as a theistic interpretation of empirical observations; the constants have been empirically observed, and from there we can reach a conclusion. Would you like to comment on whether this interpretation is acceptable?

CHT: Well, it is certainly very clear that this universe is very special. It is remarkable and highly improbable that its creation is random. So how did it happen? Well, there are several possibilities.

One possibility is that it was planned by a fantastic intelligence you might call God, who planned the universe and the laws of physics. People who don't want to believe in a spiritual being might say, "The only explanation is that we agree that it is highly improbable, but maybe there is an infinite number of universes, all having different laws of physics, and the only one that happened to turn out right is this one. Since this is the only one that turned out right, that is the reason we are here." That is, of course, just imagination, since we don't know of these universes; we can't do any scientific testing to find out if they are there. Now the other difficulty with that is, why is it that the laws of physics would change from one universe to another? We don't know what makes the laws of physics the way they are – it is a great puzzle. Maybe the simplest concept is that this was all planned by a superior intelligence somehow. However, one can make other postulates such as the existence of an infinite number of universes, or that somehow the laws of physics have to be the way they are, although we don't know why they have to be that way.

> We don't know what makes the laws of physics the way they are – it is a great puzzle. Maybe the simplest concept is that this was all planned by a superior intelligence somehow.
>
> — Townes

TDS: Now if we adopt that conception or understanding, then we could say that all scientific knowledge, or knowledge per se, could be understood as divinely inspired. In science, for example, I think there is the sense of inspiration and intuition where very wonderful ideas appear from time to time in the minds of scientists such as yourself. I remember you mentioning to me that when you discovered the laser it came all of a sudden as an inspiration or revelation, from what I would call a divine source. According to *Vedanta* – the Hindu tradition – there are three aspects of God.[2]

THE CONCEPT BEHIND LASER

The possibility of stimulating the radiation was anticipated by A. Einstein in 1917, but the devices to build them were not created till the 50s. The American physicists Charles H. Townes and A. L. Schawlow demonstrated that these devices can be built using visible light.

Atoms and molecules have determinate energetic levels, which can be low or high. Those in low energetic levels can be *excited* to high levels, generally by heating. On absorption, a quantum (a unit of energy) of electromagnetic field is captured by an atom or molecule and the energy in the light quantum is converted into atomic excitation energy (figure b). The energy in a quantum of light is equal to the product of Planck's constant, h, a natural constant, and the frequency of the light, v. The excited atom can re-emit this excitation energy in the form of a quantum of light, either spontaneously or through stimulation by the external radiation field. During spontaneous emission, the quantum is emitted in a random direction at a random phase (figure c). This occurs, for instance, in ordinary lamps, and the resultant radiation field consists of overlapping wave trains at various phases and in various directions (figure a). In most cases the sources of ordinary light which comes from atoms and excited molecules and the light emission is done in various wavelengths (and frequencies). But, if during the short instant an atom is excited, the atom is influenced by light of a certain wavelength, this atom can be stimulated to launch radiation that is in phase with the wavelength that has stimulated it (figure d). In contrast, the atoms emitted during stimulated emission are forced into phase by the radiation field. When a number of these in-phase wave trains overlap each other, the resultant radiation field propagates in the one direction with a very stable amplitude. The spectral bandwidth of the radiation is also much smaller than that of an ordinary lamp.

Two conditions must be met in order to synchronise (figure e) this stimulated atomic emission: firstly, there must be more atoms present in their higher, excited states than in the lower energy levels, i.e. there must be an inversion. The second important condition is that the radiation field is sufficiently large in order that there are more stimulated emissions than spontaneous ones.

(a)

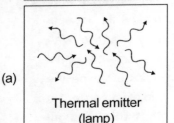

Thermal emitter (lamp)

(b)

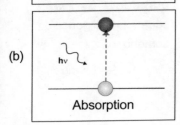

Absorption

(c)

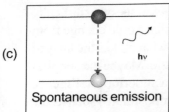

Spontaneous emission

(d)

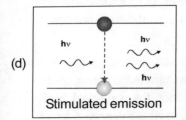

Stimulated emission

(e)

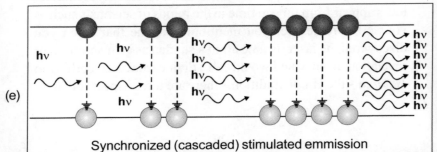

Synchronized (cascaded) stimulated emmission

The first is *Brahman,* or the impersonal all-pervading aspect. This is similar to Einstein's impersonal conception of God, as the beautiful and fantastic laws of nature – a phenomenon in nature. The second aspect is known as *Paramātmā,* which is translated as the Supersoul. *Paramātmā* is a localized aspect of God. *Paramātmā* is within every living being and is the source of inspiration and intuition. The third aspect is known as *Bhagavān,* or the Supreme Personality of Godhead. I would appreciate your comment on these aspects of God as explained in Vedanta.

CHT: Very interesting. I think we have to be very open-minded. I would say that God is everything. It is very difficult for us to define God.

TDS: Do you think some spiritual being is guiding us?

CHT: That's right. Some spiritual being or spiritual ideas are guiding us, and we simply can't conceive of them. There are many things we don't understand: What is a human? Where is a human? Are we somewhere up in the top of our head? Where is this person? How do we have free will? How can we make choices? And so on. There are many things we don't understand. There are forces in nature and within our universe that we don't understand. We have to accept the idea that they are probably there. We can feel and sense them, but we cannot understand them.

TDS: You have said that the true spirit of science is the search for truth, and that it is also meant to discover the unseen laws of nature. In this regard, you have also said that science is not necessarily materialistic. In other words, science is not to be termed as completely materialistic. Very interestingly, Karl Pribram said, "Science is spiritual" in our interview with him, which was published with the title *Science is Spiritual* in the first issue of our journal.[3] Also, you said that in the search for truth it would certainly be beneficial if scientists can incorporate spiritual principles in their scientific works. It would be good if you could elaborate on this. I'd like to mention in this connection that it would be very beneficial

> ... it would be very beneficial to incorporate principles like the role of God in scientific research, especially in connection with the study of life and its origin.
>
> — T. D. Singh

to incorporate principles like the role of God in scientific research, especially in connection with the study of life and its origin. Regarding life's origin, chemical evolutionists claim that chemical reactions as a function of the cosmic timescale are the dynamics of matter that will lead to life. They proclaim that billions of years of evolution of chemical reactions will give rise to life. In other words, the chemical evolutionists state that life or a living being is a product of chemical reactions. But this conception still remains as an idea only, and this idea could certainly be wrong.[4] I personally feel very strongly that a divine mechanism could be a more realistic model. Bringing in the concept of God's spiritual energies along with the known material energies could be more realistic. In a divine paradigm, the argument is like this: The seed of life, or to be more precise, life itself, exists as a fundamental spiritual particle. As an example, when the sperm cell of the father in which life is already present interacts and combines with the egg from the mother, the bodily form of a life particle develops. So, from the very beginning, an animated physical body grows when the life particle is present, and not the other way around - that the body has developed first and life enters later on. So, applying the argument of the *Vedantic* conception of creation, life would have to be present from the beginning. Thus the *Vedantic* conception holds that from the beginning of the existence of the Universe, not just the earth, life as a fundamental spiritual particle has existed along with the fundamental material elements and has been integral to the development of the various bodily forms that we know of today. I would appreciate your comments in this regard.

CHT: Very interesting. Well, I think it is important to recognize that from the traditional scientific viewpoint we have no idea what the probability of life is. We can be pretty sure that it happened only once on earth, because we are all related – all species on earth are related. All are built of the same type of molecules – left handed types. Left handed molecules and right handed molecules are equally valid. Why aren't there any right handed types of amino acids in protein molecules? That means life probably formed here only once, certainly not more than two or three times. The probability of the beginning of life must be very small. The Earth is a very favorable place for life to form, but it formed only once, some few billions of years ago. So, the probability is very small. How small? We don't know that. We don't know how it started. There are many puzzles, and I think we must recognize them. Some scientists say, "Well, of course, it is just chemistry. So chemicals come together, never mind how. And in any case, no problem." But they have to come together in a very special way, and we don't know the probability of that. It must be very, very small. Now, in addition to that, the idea of consciousness is strange. You see, molecules – we think of them as materialistic things. Then, what is consciousness? We have difficulty even in defining consciousness, or the conscious being. There may be other forces involved outside of what our science presently knows.

TDS: We can call them the spiritual forces.

CHT: Spiritual forces, or other forces. In physics now, we are finding more and more unknown things that we recognize must be present. For example, most of the matter in our universe that we know must be there, we can't see. We don't know what most of the matter is. We can see and detect only five percent of the matter in our universe. We don't know what the rest is. We are finding new forces in our universe, and there is no reason to think that there aren't additional forces present. So, we try hard to understand. Science is an effort to understand how the universe

What are we all about? Why are we here? What are we supposed to do? What is our life like? What does it mean? And so on. These are the most important questions, I think. If we understand the answers to these questions, they will determine very much what we must do, what we are doing and why and how we should do it. What is it all about? What is the purpose? Why is the universe here? Why are we here? ... My own view is that God has formed this universe and given us free will to be somewhat like Him, have some of His attributes, to help others and to help humanity and this universe grow – to hopefully improve and increase, and come close to God.

— Townes

works. We try hard and hope we can find out more and more and more. But we must also recognize that there is much we don't understand, and we must accept that.

TDS: Well, if life comes about only once and the conditions were rightly formed from the beginning and life is viewed as a spiritual force or other forces that was always present, then this could be in harmony with the theistic conception – God as the source of both the material energy, or force, and life.

CHT: Yes, it certainly corresponds with the theistic interpretation. That's quite correct.

TDS: At the press conference held in March this year when you won the Templeton Prize you made a profound statement: "I believe there is no long-range question more important than the purpose and meaning of our lives and of the universe."[5] Would you please elaborate on that?

CHT: Well, yes, what is more important? What are we all about? Why are we here? What are we supposed to do? What is our life like? What does it mean? And so on. These are the most important questions, I think. If we understand the answers to these questions, they will determine very much what we must do, what we are doing and why and how we should do it. What is it all about? What is the purpose? Why is the universe here? Why are we here? These are all very basic questions. I think we should ponder them more and take them very seriously, and they are the questions religion attempts to answer. My own view is that God has formed this universe and given us free will to be somewhat like Him, have some of His attributes, to help others and to help humanity and this universe grow – to hopefully improve and increase, and come close to God.

TDS: That's a wonderful viewpoint. At the news conference you also said, "If the universe has a meaning and a purpose, this must be reflected in its structure, functioning and, hence, to science."[6]

... if we see the structure of the universe as having really remarkable characteristics, it seems to suggest that there is a purpose. ... if we understand the structure and how it works very well, then that may give us some hints as to the purpose of the universe. If we understand the purpose, then that should probably say how it is structured. Those two must come close together, and this is why I say that science and religion are really quite parallel. They must converge.

— Townes

Atom

CHT: Yes, well, of course some people will argue that the universe has no purpose – it is just a random thing. No purpose at all. So what is it all about? Nothing. Nothing, and that makes life very unimportant. On the other hand, if there is a purpose and if we see the structure of the universe as having really remarkable characteristics, it seems to suggest that there is a purpose. If there is a purpose, then its structure must be closely related to the purpose. So, if we understand the structure and how it works very well, then that may give us some hints as to the purpose of the universe. If we understand the purpose, then that should probably say how it is structured. Those two must come close together, and this is why I say that science and religion are really quite parallel. They must converge. And they can influence and inform each other. The purpose and the structure and how it works must be closely related, and if we understand one very well, then hopefully we can understand the other better.

TDS: Max Born once stated that from the study of the structure of the atoms, he could appreciate the existence of a Creator - God. Is it something like this?

CHT: Well, many scientists have said that after the discovery of remarkable characteristics of this universe – the atoms and how they are made and so on – it seems so remarkable that it has to be somehow planned. Now, one can still argue that it is an accident. But, it seems to me that it is highly improbable.

TDS: You also have said, "In addition, to best understand either science or religion, we must use all of our human resources — logic, evidence (observations or experiment), carefully chosen assumptions, intuition, and faith."[7]

CHT: Well, I think to understand either science or religion, we must use all possible human resources— instinct, logic, observation, experiments, thought, and so on. We must use all avenues to understand; that is true in science. I don't think people recognize how much we use instincts in science. We use assumptions, or

> I don't think people recognize how much we use instincts in science. We use assumptions, or we might call those postulates, which are really identical to faith. ... the postulates are simply faith. And faith in science is important. Faith in religion is important. ... We have this faith and from that, we make conclusions. Both science and religion have this characteristic.
>
> — Townes

we might call those postulates, which are really identical to faith. We use all our human instincts. We can never be completely sure of anything, but we try to make the best picture we can and we try to understand as much as we can. We do and should use everything we can assemble in order to understand.

TDS: In science, we use axioms to build knowledge. For example, we use axioms in mathematics or physics. Since we have taken these axioms for granted, as valid sources of knowledge, even without the final proof, we use axioms to build knowledge. Could faith in these axioms be deemed to be the same faith religious practitioners have in their respective spiritual axioms?

CHT: Yes, you might say axioms are postulates – the assumptions we make in science. We make certain assumptions, we make certain postulates, and from these postulates we then use logic in order to decide and conclude what the results are. Now, it has been shown mathematically that we can never even prove that the postulates are self-consistent. So, the postulates are simply faith. And faith in science is important. Faith in religion is important. We have to think, "Now, what is most likely correct?" And we make these postulates. We have this faith and from that, we make conclusions. Both science and religion have this characteristic.

TDS: You have also mentioned Gödel's argument that logic also has limitations.

CHT: That's right. That was Gödel's theorem,[8] that we can never prove anything for sure. We can never prove that our postulates are self-consistent, and they may be incorrect. We have to assume they are self-consistent.

TDS: There is a statement I found from William Phillips. When he got the Nobel Prize in 1997 for his pioneering works on laser-cooled atoms, during his press conference, he said something very interesting. He said that he takes the deity personally. He said, "Einstein's God, who is really just like laws of nature, is not for me. I am strongly of the conviction that God is a person, and that is the foundation of my faith." In fact, when he received the Nobel Prize, he said, "I would like to thank so many personalities. Also, I would like to thank God because He has given us this universe and He has engaged us to study His laws."[9] So he has a profound appreciation of God as a person. I was wondering if you have any comment on this.

CHT: Well, I agree with William Phillips that God is very personal.

He has very personal interactions with us, and I think that is very important. He is not some distant thing that just created the universe and then left it alone. I think there is continuous interaction between God and this universe, especially with us personally. That is very important to our lives.

> God is very personal. ... I think there is continuous interaction between God and this universe, especially with us personally. That is very important to our lives.
>
> — Townes

TDS: This personal aspect is explained in our tradition – the Hindu *Vedantic* tradition – and is regarded as the highest aspect of God realization. The other aspect – the impersonal aspect – is also there. Just like in the USA, the President is sitting in the White House, but his power or energy is spread all over the country. Energy is the impersonal aspect, but the person is sitting there and exists as the source of the power or energy.

CHT: Interesting. God is everywhere. He influences everything but, nonetheless, each individual can have a strong personal interaction. I am sure not only in your religion but also in the Jewish and the Christian religions God is recognized as having a very strong personal effect. And I believe that and I feel it.

TDS: I think the thoughts of the major religions are in harmony, except for Buddhism – Buddhism doesn't have any conception of either the soul or God.

CHT: I also think that Hinduism and other Eastern religions have never had a big clash between science and religion. In the Western religions there has been a clash, but I think they are coming together again, and they must come together in the long run.

TDS: Yes. I think this is a very interesting development, and you rightly said that Templeton is promoting this at a very critical time.[10]

... each individual can have a strong personal interaction. I am sure not only in your religion but also in the Jewish and the Christian religions God is recognized as having a very strong personal effect. And I believe that and I feel it.

— Townes

... happiness plays a very important role in the search for meaning and purpose.

— T. D. Singh

I think it is the right time for the scientists and the religious groups to work together, and you also said this in your speech when you delivered the keynote address in "The Second World Congress for the Synthesis of Science and Religion" held in Calcutta in January 1997.[11]

CHT: I think the interactive, back-and-forth discussion between scientists and theologians and scientific and religious people – and the discussion of science and religion amongst all people – is very important. I am delighted that Templeton is sponsoring that. I think it is growing and having an important effect.

TDS: Now I just want to discuss a point about the science of happiness. During my interaction with the Metanexus for the last few years I realized that happiness and spiritual transformation have become important topics for scientific research. In terms of happiness, whenever I see you, in spite of your age, you look very enthusiastic and lively. I want to know what the secret of your happiness is.

CHT: Well, I would say I have been very fortunate. I have just had such a good time in life. In fact, I never work, you see. I just do research in physics. It is fun. But I also think that, essentially, one should not try hard to be happy, just like one shouldn't try hard to make money. You should try to do worthwhile things. If you try to do good things, then it comes automatically. Try to do the things that you think are important and good, and then if you work hard at it, you are likely to be happy.

TDS: In our tradition, happiness is called *ānanda*. The goal of life should be *ānanda*, which is a *Sanskrit* word that means blissful – the ultimate happiness. To achieve that one needs to be very optimistic in life. For example, while doing the experiment we could be optimistic that by the blessings of the Lord the experiment will be a correct one. I think being optimistic and enthusiastic stems from a divine source or principle. It happens somehow inwardly or intuitively from within from a spiritual source.

CHT: Yes, I do think that optimism is important. I think if we understand, if we feel that we are in contact with God and His will and so on, and recognize what He is trying to do and the meaning of this universe, that generates optimism.

> ... happiness is close to the personal conception of God.
>
> — T. D. Singh

TDS: I think happiness plays a very important role in the search for meaning and purpose.

CHT: Well yes, but one should not say, "My goal is to be happy." Then what one would do to be happy is perhaps to eat a lot of ice cream. That is not good. I think we should try to do good things. Live in accordance with God's will, and that will bring happiness.

TDS: Good things?

CHT: Worthwhile things. Helping people out. Helping humanity. To live in God's world with His purposes, I think that brings happiness.

TDS: In an interview with Sir Roger Penrose published in our journal last year, he said he appreciates truth, beauty and morality as higher principles of life - existing independently of the physical or mental world.[12] These are impersonal aspects of divinity, but happiness is close to the personal conception of God. Does this make sense?

CHT: Yes, yes.

Vasudeva Rao: (Henceforth **VR)**: I have one question.

CHT: Yes, what is it?

VR: You received the Nobel Prize in 1964. In the same year, you were invited to speak to the congregation at Riverside Church about science and religion. It seems to be one of the milestones in the science and religion dialogue. I can see the results of the science and religion dialogue now, but what were your impressions at that time?

CHT: Well, the reason I gave that talk was because the men's class at Riverside Church knew that I was coming to church and they knew I was a scientist. They didn't know many scientists who were coming to church. So, they asked me "Would you come and give a talk about how scientists look at religion?" I had never given such a talk, you see. They had never heard a scientist talk about this. That's how it all started. So, I gave a talk. Then it got put on the radio and was published, and then, before I knew it, I was asked to give many more talks. That was the beginning of this back-and-forth discussion. Of course, there has been some antipathy between some scientists and religious people. But, I think they must come together. That was an effort by the church to see how scientists look at religion, and I tried to give my views. That possibly had some effect, and I am delighted that I have been able to increase the discussion in this field.

TDS: One interesting note on that – the editor of the magazine was saying that when he was preparing to publish your speech on science and religion dialogue, one alumnus scientist got very upset and said, "If you publish this article, I will withdraw myself from the magazine."

CHT: Some people disagree. That's expected, but we need to be able to discuss openly and with an open mind.

TDS: What do you think that could be considered as landmarks within the science-religion dialogue?

CHT: I can't think of any specific landmarks, although I do think there has been considerable growth in that discussion. Maybe there are some landmarks such as the recognition by scientists about how special this universe is. That's happened during the past one or two decades. More and more scientists realize that it is very, very unusual. In this universe – it is remarkable that the laws of physics turned out the way they did. Ideas like that are coming to fruition. I think that is very important.

TDS: I would say one of the landmarks should be Templeton's contribution. He is facilitating this dialogue in a big way.

CHT: I agree. I think his contribution is very important. I agree.

TDS: Also, you are rightfully the first person – a scientist, Nobel laureate, physicist and Templeton laureate. We are all fortunate that you have done such wonderful service that warrants such accolades.

CHT: I am very pleased to be able to do whatever I can.

VR: What do you think might be the next important breakthrough in the science and religion dialogue?

CHT: Well, who knows? The new things are the things we don't know. The new ideas are the things we don't know now, but if one can say where they are likely to come from, I think science, such as physics, astronomy, and biology are most likely to give us additional insight, and understanding. Perhaps we will improve our understanding of the function of the brain. And free will – how in the world do we have free will? Free will is contrary to our

I think science, such as physics, astronomy, and biology are most likely to give us additional insight, and understanding. Perhaps we will improve our understanding of the function of the brain. And free will — how in the world do we have free will? Free will is contrary to our scientific laws at the moment. We think we have free will. And what is this person? Where is the person? What is it? How does the brain work?

— Townes

scientific laws at the moment. We think we have free will. And what is this person? Where is the person? What is it? How does the brain work? And so on. If we can understand that, then we may make great progress. I think biology may make many possible contributions, but we will have to work hard to try and understand the origin of our universe, the nature of our universe, the unknown forces that we haven't discovered yet and so on. These are the things that physics and astronomy will hopefully help us learn about. I believe there are many discoveries to work on, and I am hopeful we will understand more and more.

TDS: I understand that you will be giving the keynote address at the upcoming annual conference of Metanexus Institute at Philadelphia in June. I will also be participating in that conference and I look forward to seeing you there again. Metanexus has done a

Townes and his wife Frances

wonderful job for promoting dialogue between science and religion by establishing its Local Societies Initiative (LSI) around the world.[13] I feel fortunate to be a part of this program.

CHT: Yes. Well, I hope I can do a reasonable job.

TDS: I am sure your words of wisdom will inspire everyone. Prof. Townes, I have really enjoyed our discussion. Thank you very much.

CHT: Okay, it was nice to see you, and I will see you again in Philadelphia.

TDS: Yes. Please give my regards to your good wife, Frances.

———

Notes and References

1. Refer *Savijñānam – Scientific Exploration for a Spiritual Paradigm*, Journal of the Bhaktivedanta Institute, Kolkata, 2003, vol.2, p. 79.

2. A.C. Bhaktivedanta Swami Śrīla Prabhupāda, *Śrīmadbhāgavatam*, Canto 1, Ch. 2 Verse 11, Bhaktivedanta Book Trust, Bombay, 1987, p.103.

3. T. D. Singh & Karl H. Pribram, "Science is Spiritual", *Savijñānam – Scientific Exploration for a Spiritual Paradigm*, Vol.1, Kolkata, 2002, pp. 31-39.

4. Please refer to T. D. Singh's book *Life, Matter and their Interactions*, Kolkata, 2006 for detailed account on origin of life scenario.

5. Statement by Charles Hard Townes, The Templeton Prize News Conference, March 9, 2005. web: http://www.templetonprize.org/townes_statement.html

6. *Ibid.*

7. *Ibid.*

8. For Gödel's theorem, refer: Ernest Nagel & James R. Newman, *Gödel's Proof*, New York & London, 2001; Also refer Rebecca Goldstein, *Incompleteness: The Proof and Paradox of Kurt Gödel*, 2005.

9. Refer William Phillips Nobel Lecture, "Laser Cooling and Trapping of Neutral Atoms," Dec 8, 1997.

10. Refer www.templeton.org

11. *Thoughts on Synthesis of Science and Religion*, eds. T. D. Singh and Samaresh Bandyopadhyay, Calcutta, 2001, pp. 91-114.

12. *Science, Spirituality and the Nature of Reality*, A discussion between Sir Roger Penrose and Dr. T. D. Singh, Kolkata, 2005.

13. Refer www.metanexus.net

Laser Cooling of Atoms
and
The Role of a Personal God

Prof. Phillips' contribution of developing techniques for cooling and trapping of neutral atoms using lasers has opened up a new area of study of atoms and atomic gases. Because the motion of atoms can be slowed down considerably using this technique, designs of much more precise atomic clocks have become possible. This has an application in high-speed communications and navigation using the Global Positioning System (GPS) which require very precise timing. But what is most unique about Prof. Phillips is that besides being a well-known scientist, he also has a deep commitment in religious values. His deep scientific knowledge driven by a profound religious commitment certainly makes his wisdom much sharper than the sharp laser beams.

*P*rof. William D. Phillips has been a leading researcher in the field of laser cooling of atoms at the National Institute of Standards and Technology (NIST), Maryland since 1978, and was elected to the National Academy of Sciences in 1997. He is internationally known for advancing basic knowledge and new techniques to chill atoms to extremely low temperatures. His experiments demonstrated that a beam of neutral atoms could be slowed down and cooled with radiation pressure from a laser and that atoms cooled by lasers could reach much lower temperatures than had been predicted theoretically. This work paved the way for scientists to create Bose-Einstein condensation, an exotic new form of matter in which atoms all fall into their lowest levels and merge into a single quantum state. In 1997 Dr. Phillips received the Nobel Prize in Physics with Claude Cohen Tannoudji and Steven Chu for developing methods to cool and trap atoms with laser light. Despite all these scientific achievements Dr. Phillips also has firm faith in the existence of a personal God; Einstein's God is not sufficient for him.

Dr. T. D. Singh, who himself is a scientist as well as a spiritualist in the Bhaktivedanta tradition of India and a pioneer in advancing dialogue between science and religion, met him in his office at NIST, Maryland. The following dialogue, "Laser Cooling of atoms and the Role of a Personal God" is a significant discussion between William Phillips and T. D. Singh held at the National Institute of Standards and Technology (NIST), Gaithersburg, USA on June 11, 2005, after official working hours.

೮෪

William D. Phillips (Henceforth **WDP**): Welcome. I hope you didn't have much difficulty in reaching my office.

T. D. Singh (Henceforth **TDS**): Thank you Prof. Phillips. We didn't have any difficulty to come to your office. Your direction was perfect. I'm happy to see you. This is the book on the discussion I had with Prof. Penrose. (Shows book.) I sent you a copy.[1]

WDP: Yes, I received it. It is very nice.

TDS: I visited Prof. Townes last month in his office at U.C. Berkeley. He is a wonderful person. I've known him for over 20 years. He is not only a great scientist but also a deeply religious person. I am very happy that he won the Templeton Prize this year. At his office we had a discussion centered on the close connection between science and religion. During our conversation, I mentioned that I would be seeing you next month. He spoke very highly of you.

WDP: It was such a great joy to know that Charlie (Charles Townes) won the Templeton Prize this year.

TDS: Recently he also gave the keynote address in Philadelphia on the convergence of science and religion at the annual conference organized by the Metanexus Institution on June 4th. He is celebrating his 90th birthday in October at Berkeley, and I thought you might be attending.

WDP: Yes, I'm not only going, I'm co-chairing the symposium that is part of his 90th birthday celebrations. Raymond Chiao, who is one of his colleagues at the University of California at Berkeley, and myself are the co-chairs of the symposium. The Templeton Foundation is one of the sponsors for symposium marking Charlie's 90th birthday, and we're looking forward to a wonderful celebration.[2]

TDS: Yes, I met him at the recent Metanexus conference where he asked me whether I was coming to join his 90th birthday celebrations. (Both laugh.) When I organized the Second World Congress for the Synthesis of Science and Religion in Calcutta in January 1997, I was so happy that he could come and give the keynote address. Over 2,000 scientists and religious leaders from around the world participated in that conference.[3] The conference was organized on the occasion of the centennial birthday of my spiritual master, Srila A.C. Bhaktivedanta Swami Prabhupada, one of the greatest exponents of *Vedic* culture in the 20th century. Prof. Townes is just as active now as he was eight years ago. He is extremely healthy and energetic. The Lord must have blessed him.

WDP: Yes, he's elderly but very vigorous. I just wish that even at the age of 80 I could be half as active as he is at the age of 90. He's really quite remarkable, and his wife, who is almost the same age, is also very active.

TDS: Let me introduce my friends who came with me today. This is Vasudev Rao, my secretary. He has done his masters degree in Computer Science from the Indian Institute of Technology (IIT), Kanpur. This is Abhishek Tiwari, my student who is doing a Ph.D. in Computer Science at the University of Illinois, Urbana-Champaign; next to him is Mr. Luciano Nonino who has just finished his studies in Economics and is working in the United States. He is an Italian and very religious. They are all very interested in the search for the meaning of life and the science of God. They are all helping me in my work on the dialogue between science and religion.

WDP: Part of my heritage is Italian as well.

TDS: Yes, I read that your mother is Italian.

WDP: My mother was born in the southern part of Italy, near the city of Potenza.

TDS: We came all the way from California to Philadelphia to attend the annual Metanexus conference. The conference was over a few days ago and we drove here from Philadelphia.

WDP: So you've been associated with Metanexus?

TDS: Yes, I have been part of the worldwide Local Societies Initiative (LSI) program of Metanexus for the last two years.[4]

WDP: And now you have come all the way from Philadelphia to see me. What motivated you to interview me?

TDS: Well, on reading your biography, it is very inspiring to note that you are not only a pioneering scientist but also a highly religious person. There are not too many scientists in the world like you. I was very impressed with your background, especially your growing up – the human side of you – and the tremendous amount of respect you have for your parents, your

> I always thought of religion as being a natural part of life.
>
> — Phillips

deep commitment to religious values, and your duties in the church. It is something very exemplary. What do you think are some of the important factors that have contributed to your fascinating life?

WDP: Certainly the way I was brought up by my parents contributed a great deal to my religious thought because religion was always a part of our lives. We always gave thanks before meals and my parents taught me to pray every day. We always went to church, and we were very much involved in the life of the church – not just going to church on Sundays, but also being involved in other activities of the church. Many aspects of faith and church were just a part of life for me. It was something that was as much a part of life as other things were. Growing up in that kind of environment obviously had a big effect on me. I always thought of religion as being a natural part of life.

TDS: You also said that you learned from childhood to respect other people, cultures and faiths from your parents. I think that is a wonderful quality that can ultimately foster humility and open-mindedness.

WDP: Yes, I think it's something that children ought to be taught. It's something that children have to learn, and it's very important for us to teach our children in this way. Just as we can teach our children to be very accepting and respectful of other people, it is of course possible to teach them the opposite. I think a great deal of difficulty that we have in the world is from people who have been taught from an early age not to respect people of all faiths and backgrounds. But I was taught by my parents that that is the right way – to respect everyone.

TDS: A good family environment plays a very important role in human culture. It is important for the parents to teach their children to respect people of other cultures and communities, to cultivate a culture of unity in diversity. I think if we all act like that then it will be a lot easier to have world peace.

WDP: Absolutely. One of the things that motivated my parents to teach us in that way was the experience my mother had as a little girl coming from Italy to the United States. This may be particularly interesting to your colleague Luciano, who also comes from Italy. My mother came to the United States from the southern part of Italy when she was eight years old, and she suffered a great deal of persecution because she was different from the other people. It was a time when a lot of people were immigrating into the United States from many different countries. The people in the United States at that time were uncomfortable with people who seemed somewhat different or didn't speak English. My mother experienced that kind of intolerance herself, and I think that experience convinced her that she would never repeat that kind of behavior toward others. She would be sure to teach her children to always respect other people and never to treat anyone the way she had been treated. I think it takes a very special sort of person to have been treated with intolerance and to react by trying to ensure that no

> ... it takes a very special sort of person to have been treated with intolerance and to react by trying to ensure that no one else ever gets treated that way. I'm afraid that when some people are treated badly, their natural reaction is to treat others badly.
>
> — Phillips

one else ever gets treated that way. I'm afraid that when some people are treated badly, their natural reaction is to treat others badly. But her reaction was completely different. Her reaction was to be sure to do whatever she could to see that other people were not treated badly.

TDS: This quality is very wonderful. Not many people in the world today behave in this way. Your mother must have been very pious.

WDP: I hope that many people do behave this way, but certainly not all people do.

TDS: One of the things that is very interesting about your life is that you talk about the power of prayer. I find this is extremely interesting for a scientist. In your biography you mention that you prayed for the birth of a younger brother, and confirmation came after your prayer.

In scientific research, you have done pioneering research in laser cooling of atoms. In the process of your experimentation or through receiving certain concepts in that direction did you also get some kind of inspiration or direction through prayer?

WDP: Well, my concept of the nature and the importance of prayer have changed a great deal since I was a child. Let me recount the story of how my sister and I prayed for a brother, or a sibling. When my parents did have my brother, we were very thankful, believing that it was in answer to our prayer. I have said that this event confirmed the power of prayer for me, but from the point of view of a child. I'm not sure that I have the same idea about the nature and importance of prayer today. For example, today there are certain things that I don't pray for that I did pray for as a child. I do not pray for things that will benefit me materially. I feel that those kinds of things are not proper to pray for. I pray for other people, for the welfare of others and for greater understanding of myself, not for material things. I also remember that as a child I was very impressed by the story of Solomon in the Bible. Solomon was a king of Israel, and he was given the

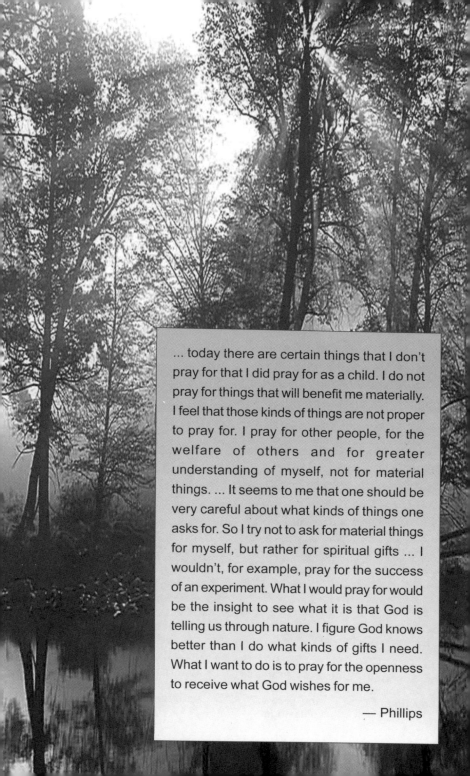

... today there are certain things that I don't pray for that I did pray for as a child. I do not pray for things that will benefit me materially. I feel that those kinds of things are not proper to pray for. I pray for other people, for the welfare of others and for greater understanding of myself, not for material things. ... It seems to me that one should be very careful about what kinds of things one asks for. So I try not to ask for material things for myself, but rather for spiritual gifts ... I wouldn't, for example, pray for the success of an experiment. What I would pray for would be the insight to see what it is that God is telling us through nature. I figure God knows better than I do what kinds of gifts I need. What I want to do is to pray for the openness to receive what God wishes for me.

— Phillips

Prayer is a natural function of the soul, the life particle that animates living bodies and it becomes spontaneously visible when one is in danger or difficulty, as for instance, during the danger in Appollo mission-13.

Danger in Appollo 13: Pope Paul VI requested all the people of the earth to pray for the safe return of the astronauts.

... the true religious person, a *vaishnava*, never asks for anything to benefit himself, but always prays for the well-being of others. It is said, *para-dukha-dukhi*: meaning he feels unhappy because of the unhappiness of others.

— T. D. Singh

Brahma prays to the Supreme Lord for spiritual knowledge

The exalted devotee Prahlada Maharaja prays for the Lord's blessings

Pope John Paul II absorbed in prayer

Queen Kunti begs the Lord for more calamities because these would help her remember Him more and more

opportunity to ask for a gift from God. He could ask for any number of things, but what he asked for was wisdom. It seems to me that one should be very careful about what kinds of things one asks for. So I try not to ask for material things for myself, but rather for spiritual gifts, and with the hope that if I have spiritual gifts then everything else will come. Even if I don't get material gifts, it doesn't really matter as long as I have the spiritual gifts. I wouldn't, for example, pray for the success of an experiment. What I would pray for would be the insight to see what it is that God is telling us through nature. I figure God knows better than I do what kinds of gifts I need. What I want to do is to pray for the openness to receive what God wishes for me.

TDS: You have wonderful devotional qualities. There is a great similarity in our *Vaishnava* tradition of India. The *Vaishnava* tradition is part of Hinduism. *Vaishnavism* says that the true religious person, a *vaishnava*, never asks for anything to benefit himself, but always prays for the well-being of others. It is said, *para-duḥkha-duḥkhī*: meaning he feels unhappy because of the unhappiness of others. In that way, it is very similar to your perspective.

WDP: It sounds very similar, and I'm sure that we can learn a great deal from that kind of wisdom.

TDS: I was very impressed to read that you expressed your appreciation of God's gifts during the press conference when you received the Nobel Prize in 1997. You said, "I thank individual personalities, but I also thank God for giving us the universe for our exploration and insights." I mentioned this to Charles Townes and he too appreciated it. How did this intuition and spontaneous feeling come to you?

WDP: Well, it was something that just came to me. Getting a Nobel Prize was not something I had imagined would happen to me, and I was just so stunned by what a wonderful thing it was. I think, in any career when something wonderful happens to you,

> ... it seems to us as scientists – and I say this sort of light-heartedly – that the world is so wonderful that it must have been that God created this world just so we can have so much fun. The world is so interesting that it's hard to escape the idea that God made the world so interesting in order to provide pleasure to people through exploring it.
>
> — Phillips

you want to say thanks. If you're a religious person, you want to give thanks for the good things that happen to you. Perhaps I didn't say it quite that way. I gave thanks more for the wonderful world that had allowed all of these things to happen. Of course, in my mind I was also giving thanks for the wonderful thing that had happened to me, but without having such an intriguing and interesting world to live in, none of these other good things would have happened.

Let me mention an important point. Getting a Nobel Prize is a wonderful thing, but I don't believe it's a sort of thing that one should work toward. What one should work towards is searching for understanding, and if that new understanding leads to some kind of recognition like a Nobel Prize, then so much the better. The important thing is to work to get that new understanding. And God has given us a world in which we can do that, which is wonderful. Especially for those of us who have chosen science as a career, it gives us so much fulfillment to be able to explore a world that has so much richness. Sometimes it seems to us as scientists – and I say this sort of light-heartedly – that the world is so wonderful that it must have been that God created this world just so we can have so much fun. The world is so interesting that it's hard to escape the idea that God made the world so interesting in order to provide pleasure to people through exploring it. And you could say this about some of the other things. The world is so

> It is mentioned in our Vedantic literature that this world was created by the Lord in order to fulfill the desires of the living entities who wished to have material pleasure. However, there is a divine plan behind this whole manifestation – it is designed in such a manner that a living being can elevate his consciousness and revive his love of God while experiencing this world. Moreover, the importance of human life is emphasized because consciousness and free will are more fully developed in the human form of life than in any other forms of life.
>
> — T. D. Singh

beautiful that it must be that God created that beauty to provide pleasure to creatures of this world. I think the interesting nature of the world as being something that is on the same level as the beauty of the world.

TDS: You appreciate the gifts of God in a very devotional way. It is mentioned in our Vedantic literature that this world was created by the Lord in order to fulfill the desires of the living entities who wished to have material pleasure. However, there is a divine plan behind this whole manifestation – it is designed in such a manner that a living being can elevate his consciousness and revive his love of God while experiencing this world. Moreover, the importance of human life is emphasized because consciousness and free will are more fully developed in the human form of life than in any other forms of life.

Also, one very important concept that you have stated is that Einstein's God lies within the laws of nature, but you say that is not your conception – rather, you say your conception is of a personal God.

WDP: Absolutely. Sometimes people talk about Einstein's God as being an impersonal God. In fact, Einstein at times said that he did not believe in the idea of a personal God. So first of all, let me say that I very much believe in the idea of a personal God. Charlie Townes believes in a personal God. But if you look at some of the things that Einstein said, I wonder if he didn't actually have the idea of a personal God, since he talked about God in a very personal way. When he was writing intellectually about the mysterious, he insisted that God was not personal, but when he talked in a casual way about God, he talked about God in a very personal way. In talking about quantum mechanics, for example, he said, "I can't believe that God plays dice." Now that's a very personal thing to say, so I'm not so sure of whether or not deep down in his mind Einstein really did have a more personal idea about God than he was willing to say in a formal way. In fact, another time he said he was surprised by the way in which nature worked. He said something like, "I wonder what the old man is thinking," referring to God. That is not an impersonal way of talking about God. So I'm not so sure about Einstein being so impersonal in his idea about God. Certainly people like myself and Charlie Townes will be very firm in saying that our God is very personal.

TDS: Maybe Einstein kept some thoughts a little hidden.

WDP: Maybe he did keep some thoughts a little hidden. Maybe he didn't fully admit to himself the way he felt about God.

TDS: He said that his conception of God was very much influenced by Spinoza's philosophy. It is a monistic conception, and probably he was very influenced in that direction. In our Vedic tradition it is said that there are three aspects of God.[5] One is impersonal or universal pervasiveness – in Sanskrit it is called the *Brahman* aspect of God. It is the most commonly appreciated aspect where one perceives God as an impersonal all-pervading concept, such as many scientists see the laws of nature. The second is called the *Paramātmā* aspect of God. *Paramātmā* is the localized and in-dwelling personal aspect of God who guides each living being

I very much believe in the idea of a personal
God. ... Certainly people like myself and
Charlie Townes will be very firm in saying that
our God is very personal.

— Phillips

Einstein could only appreciate the impersonal aspect of God. In this conception, there is a definite feeling of awe and reverence when looking at the majesty of nature and the universe. From the Vedantic perspective, however, the Personality aspect of God is most important. This does not imply that the concept is anthropomorphic. It is not that we give a human shape or characteristic to a god or anything whimsically. Rather it is the revelation of God Himself to self-realized transcendentalists.

— T. D. Singh

from within. The third aspect is *Bhagavān*. *Bhagavān* means the Supreme Person, the personal aspect of the Lord – the Supreme Personality of God – whom we are meant to have a relationship with. So this realization of the personal aspect, called *Bhagavān,* is the highest. We can illustrate this with a metaphor. You have the President sitting in the White House, but his power or impersonal energy is spread throughout the country. Similarly, I think that one additional aspect in the Vedic tradition is the *Paramātmā*, also called the Supersoul, which is within every living being, and also within the atom. The *Paramātmā* guides the individual being in a very personal way.

In the history of science, most scientists are influenced by the impersonal concept of God. This is generally due to misconceptions about the nature of the personal aspect of God being steeped in pantheism or anthropomorphism. Thus Einstein could only appreciate the impersonal aspect of God. In this conception, there is a definite feeling of awe and reverence when looking at the majesty of nature and the universe. From the Vedantic perspective, however, the Personality aspect of God is most important. This does not imply that the concept is anthropomorphic. It is not that we give a human shape or characteristic to a god or anything whimsically. Rather it is the revelation of God Himself to self-realized transcendentalists. A divine maxim is found in the *Śrīmad Bhāgavatam*⁶ stating that the cause exists certainly in its effect as well. Following this argument, since we all experience very clearly that all developed living beings have individual personalities, it is certainly conceivable that the Supreme source of all must also possess personality.

When I read your background, I felt very strongly that your experience of relating with God is quite similar to what we have in the *Vaishnava* culture. You relate with God as a Supreme Person. In this regard, you and Charles Townes stand out among the modern prominent scientists. Although you are Christians, the similarity between *Vaishnavism* and Christianity is very striking in this regard.

WDP: In fact, my impression is that the idea of a personal God is a very conventional viewpoint, whether one is a Christian or a Hindu, or belonging to many of the world's great religions. I think that people often think about the divine presence as being very personal. But generally this question often arises: What about scientists? Do scientists take more to Einstein's point of view, or are scientists more traditional? Well, of course, as with anything else, you have a whole range. You have scientists who claim that they are atheists, you have scientists who believe in Einstein's God, and you have scientists who will say they believe in a personal God. But I think that there is a misconception that scientists tend not to have the kind of beliefs that we've been talking about. In fact, there are plenty of scientists like myself and Charlie Townes who believe in a personal God.

I think it is a mistake to believe that in general scientists do not have these kinds of beliefs. Especially in the United States, there has been a perception of conflict between science on the one hand and traditional religious faith on the other, so that people think scientists in general do not have traditional religious faith. It's not true. My church has many scientists who are its members. I'll tell you a story, which I'm not sure I have written up. When my daughter went to high school, she met many new friends, and one of her new friends told her, "My mother is a scientist, so of course she is an atheist," and my daughter told her friend, "Well if you went to my church, you wouldn't be able to walk across the fellowship hall after the worship service without running into half a dozen physicists." So this popular notion that scientists are naturally going to be atheists is simply wrong, and is known to be wrong by almost anybody who has experience of knowing enough scientists or knowing enough church-going people to see the range of experience these people have. I know many scientists who have very traditional, conventional religious views. Of course, I know scientists who are atheists, and I know scientists who simply aren't sure. So, I don't think that I'm so unusual. In fact, when I talk about science and faith, that's one of the main things that I try

Copernicus
(1473-1543)

Kepler
(1571-1630)

Robert Boyle
(1627-1691)

Most of the scientists who changed the course of humanity and made profound contributions to shape our worldview had some conception of God. Shown below is a small sample.

Mendel
(1822-1884)

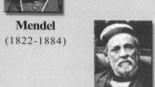

Pasteur
(1822-1895)

B. Riemann
(1826- 1866)

Newton
(1642-1727)

Faraday
(1791-1867)

Planck
(1858-1947)

Einstein
(1879-1955)

Maxwell
(1831-1879)

Mendeléev
(1834-1907)

Max Born
(1882-1970)

Ramanujan
(1887-1920)

Heisenberg
(1901-1976)

... this popular notion that scientists are naturally going to be atheists is simply wrong, and is known to be wrong by almost anybody who has experience of knowing enough scientists ...

— Phillips

> ... there is nothing unusual about a scientist who is also a person of faith in a very conventional way. ... I wish that more people understood that this was the case – that there is no contradiction between being a serious scientist and being a person who is serious about religious faith.
>
> — Phillips

to get across as a message, that there is nothing unusual about a scientist who is also a person of faith in a very conventional way. Just as I know many scientists who are Christians in very traditional ways; there are Jewish scientists who are traditional in their religious faith. Through the Science and the Spiritual Quest research program, which you know about, I have also met Buddhists and Hindus and other scientists who are very traditional. I know scientists in many of the faiths of the world who are very traditional in their religious beliefs. I wish that more people understood that this was the case – that there is no contradiction between being a serious scientist and being a person who is serious about religious faith.

TDS: Well, I find this conflict between science and religious principles, or science and spirituality mainly in the Western world. Just like in the United States you have this conflict between the Darwinian evolutionists and the creationists, or intelligent design theorists. Nowadays, this conflict is very much in the limelight.

WDP: Yes, it is.

TDS: But in the Eastern countries like India we don't have much conflict because the field of science and the field of religious principles are quite distinct and at the same time are complementary to each other. The dialogue between science and religion is an important part and should definitely create a better atmosphere in the West also. In fact we all know that the interest of this dialogue is increasing very fast around the world.

WDP: I think that's right. I don't know as much as I wish I did about Eastern religions. But one of the features of Eastern religions that I think may be important in this regard is the integration of religion with life. I think that in the East there is a more complete integration of religious faith with life than in the West. In the West we have tended to separate the religious part of our life from the business and family parts of our life, so that we don't seem to put all these things together in a single package. I remember when I was at Oxford and I spent a year there I remember one of the nice things about being in a college like Oxford is that you come in contact with people from many different intellectual disciplines. I had a number of conversations with a scholar whose specialty was the study of Buddhism, and he told me that when Western scholars first began to study Buddhism they would ask questions about what the nature of their beliefs was. The Buddhists didn't know how to answer that question because the nature of their beliefs was just the way they lived – it wasn't a separate question. If you would ask a Christian what are the things that you believe as a Christian, well you can think of the Apostles' Creed or the Nicene Creed or something like it. But if you ask a Buddhist what principles he believes in as a Buddhist, he will find that confusing because it is too well integrated with everything. This is the way the scholars explained it to me: that Buddhism was so well integrated into everything, and I think the same is true in the Hindu faith – there is integration and this integration is lacking in the West.

> ... in the East there is a more complete integration of religious faith with life than in the West. In the West we have tended to separate the religious part of our life from the business and family parts of our life, so that we don't seem to put all these things together in a single package.
>
> — Phillips

> In the *Vedantic* tradition there is a clear distinction between the spiritual and the material. ... Scientific study of matter is *apara-vidya* whereas knowledge of the science of God is *para-vidya*. The lower form of knowledge will lead to the understanding of the existence of higher knowledge, *para-vidya*. Just like when Max Born said, "From the knowledge of the atoms, I could appreciate the existence of a Creator."
>
> — T. D. Singh

TDS: Yes. In the *Vedantic* tradition there is a clear distinction between the spiritual and the material. In Sanskrit, the two are called *para-vidya* and *apara-vidya*. *Para-vidya* is higher knowledge, which includes spiritual values and life's meaning. *Para* means higher. The other component is physical knowledge, called *apara-vidya*, which means the lower form of knowledge. Both these are legitimate fields of knowledge, but the conclusion is that the study of the *apara-vidya* ultimately should lead to *para-vidya*. Scientific study of matter is *apara-vidya* whereas knowledge of the science of God is *para-vidya*. The lower form of knowledge should lead to the understanding of the existence of higher knowledge, *para-vidya*. Just like when Max Born said, "I saw in it (the atom) the key to the deepest secret of nature, and it revealed to me the greatness of creation and the Creator." In a way, knowing the domain of each field leads to integration. So in the *Vedantic* tradition we are not much concerned about the apparent conflict, the domains are clear.

WDP: Yes, in fact I believe that for most people the conflict is often seen in media reports. But they do not experience that kind of conflict in their own lives. I think the conflict is something that makes for good press – interesting stories – but in fact it is not in the mainstream of thought. Even among people of religious faith or among scientists in the United States, the conflict model represents only a small fraction of either the scientists or people of religious faith. I think that majority of the people do not see this as being a problem. Certainly most of the people I encounter in the church or in the scientific world don't see this as being a problem. The problem comes when you have people of religious faith who have a misconception that all scientists are atheists and materialists and have no connection to spiritual thinking. Or, scientists who believe that all people of religious faith are fools because they believe in things that are manifestly not true. I think that only a few people on either side have this kind of belief.

TDS: In relation to the concept of God, many scientists today express that the universe is fine-tuned. Prof. Townes said that the universe is very special: "If the mass of the electrons were slightly a different value, the universe would have been quite different than what we have today."[7] This is also called the anthropic principle. What is your view on this?

WDP: Yes, so let me say something. This is a subject that is very popular these days. When I look at that sort of situation, the one that Townes has described and a lot of other people have talked about, it certainly seems to me that when you see how fine-tuned the universe is, that it is a natural conclusion to conclude this was a universe that was designed so that life might develop, so that it would have the potential for all sorts of wonderful things to happen. In fact, I believe that's the case. I believe that the universe was designed in terms of the fundamental constants, that things were put into the universe when it was created and that the Creator gave us a universe that had the potential to produce creatures like us. Why? Why would our Creator have given the universe the potential for creatures like us to develop? I believe it's because God wanted to have personal relationships. This goes back to the idea of believing in a personal God. Not just God as a personality, but that God wants to have personal relationships with the creatures of the universe. That is my belief.

... it certainly seems to me that when you see how fine-tuned the universe is, that it is a natural conclusion to conclude this was a universe that was designed so that life might develop, so that it would have the potential for all sorts of wonderful things to happen. In fact, I believe that's the case. I believe that the universe was designed in terms of the fundamental constants, that things were put into the universe when it was created and that the Creator gave us a universe that had the potential to produce creatures like us. Why? Why would our Creator have given the universe the potential for creatures like us to develop? I believe it's because God wanted to have personal relationships. This goes back to the idea of believing in a personal God. Not just God as a personality, but that God wants to have personal relationships with the creatures of the universe.

— Phillips

At the same time, I want to be very careful to say that I don't believe that this understanding of the special nature of the universe is in any way a proof of the existence of God. It's easy to come up with other explanations for why the universe is the way it is. You take the modern theories of cosmology and the inflationary universe, and many of these theories provide for there being multiple copies of the universe, which may or may not have different values of fundamental constants. I don't know if these theories are correct or not, but they are certainly reasonable. According to these theories, there may be a near-infinite number of other universes that have different values of fundamental constants in which there are no people, or in which there are not even any galaxies because the universe had to be fine-tuned simply to produce stars and galaxies. The apparently special creation that produced a universe that is as fine-tuned as ours may simply be an illusion, because, of course, we must live in a universe that supports life. Sometimes people talk about the anthropic principle as simply expressing that the reason why the values of the fundamental constants are what they are is simply because if they weren't, we simply wouldn't have been here to ask the question. It says nothing about God. While for me, I certainly believe that that is the reason why things are the way they are, I have to recognize that it doesn't constitute a proof. I think that a belief in God is a matter of faith, not a matter of scientific proof. And that's why we call it religious faith. I don't believe there is a scientist who can come up with a way, on scientific grounds, of convincing somebody who doesn't want to be convinced.

TDS: This is a very interesting comment. Science cannot prove or disprove the existence of God. However, from the observations of the cosmic laboratory, a thoughtful person especially a scientist can develop a genuine faith in God. People who have faith in God have faith in the teachings of scriptures and saintly scholars. Charles Townes often points out that faith is common for both science and religion.

WDP: Absolutely. This is something that I think a lot of people do not understand. Even if scientists don't have religious faith, they must have scientific faith. Einstein was very clear about this. He said that we make the assumption that the universe is ordered as a matter of faith. We couldn't do science if we didn't believe that the universe had an order – we couldn't be scientists. On the other hand, we confirm that faith in science with the orderliness of the universe when we see that things consistently come out to be the same.

I was recently in Mexico and was visiting some of the old temples and pyramids they have there, going to the museums and learning about some of the ancient people there. What I learned, or what I was told, was that some of the ancient people there did not have any confidence that the universe would continue to be the way it has always been. In other words, simply the fact that the sun had come up every morning in all their experience, did not give them confidence that it was going to continue to do so. As a result, they had to continually perform religious acts in order to ensure that the sun would come up. Today, our scientific understanding of that is our understanding of the laws of nature. We know that the sun is going to come up tomorrow morning because we understand the nature of physical law, and we believe in a law of consistency. It is also a religious principle. The religious principle is that God is faithful; God will continue to provide for us in the way that he has provided for us in the past. That faithfulness, that unchangeability of God is a belief that is related to the scientific idea of the consistency of physical law. Now, of course you can believe in the consistency of physical laws without believing in God, but as a religious person I believe in God's faithfulness, and as a scientific person I believe in the consistency of physical law. I believe there is connection between the two.

TDS: Your point on the personal connection or personal relationship with God seems very significant. This is emphasized in our tradition called *Bhakti*. *Bhakti* means a loving devotional relationship with

Bhakti means a loving devotional relationship with God and is the highest attainment in realizing God - it is not only the end but it is also the means. Subsequently if there is a personal relationship of this level then one will know about the meaning and purpose of life, why we are here, why God has created us and given us special blessings. He wants us to have a personal relationship.

— T. D. Singh

God and is the highest attainment in realizing God - it is not only the end but it is also the means. Subsequently if there is a personal relationship of this level then one will know about the meaning and purpose of life, why we are here, why God has created us and given us special blessings. He wants us to have a personal relationship.

WDP: Exactly. I couldn't agree more. I think that is exactly what God wants from us. I think that what God wants from us is to have a personal relationship with Him and to have good personal relationships with each other. That's why we're here. Maybe John put it better when he said, "As creatures of God our job is to have good relationships with the other creatures of God, with each other." So I agree with you. I think that the relationship God wants us to have with Him is a kind of model.

... that is exactly what God wants from us. I think that what God wants from us is to have a personal relationship with Him and to have good personal relationships with each other. That's why we're here. ... So I agree with you. I think that the relationship God wants us to have with Him is a kind of model.... It models for us the kinds of relationships we ought to have with each other.

— Phillips

TDS: This is very significant.

WDP: Exactly. It models for us the kinds of relationships we ought to have with each other. It teaches us about those kinds of relationships.

TDS: You have experienced many varieties of experimental worlds — growing up in life, in high school, in college and as a scientist. Do these experiences involve some kind of creativity, inspiration or divine guidance?

WDP: Well, yes, creativity is a very difficult concept to pin down. People often wonder what it is that fosters creativity. You see creativity in different areas – there is scientific creativity, artistic creativity, musical creativity and literary creativity. So I ask myself if I have been a very creative person. When I think about comparing myself with someone like Charlie Townes, I don't think I have been very creative. I think I've worked really hard. When I look at Charlie thinking about his concepts, his getting a flash of insight that one could use stimulated emission to make a new source of radiation. I guess I have never felt that kind of thing. What I have felt more is that I have worked really hard and tried to be open to what nature or God is telling us. In that regard, I remember a story that was told – I'm not sure who the scientist was, but I think it was Joseph Henry. Some people went to see this scientist. They wanted to invite him to be the head of an institution. They went to see him in his laboratory and he was embarking on an experiment, so he gathered them together and said, "We're about to do an experiment." He said, "What we're doing, when we're doing an experiment, is asking God questions, and now what we're going to do is we're going to pray that we will be able to understand the answer." So in a certain sense, when you work in the lab, that's what you are doing. You're asking God questions, and what you are hoping is that you will have enough wisdom and insight to understand what the answer is. I

What we're doing, when we're doing an experiment, is asking God questions, and now what we're going to do is we're going to pray that we will be able to understand the answer.

think that God has given me the great gift that a few times I have been able to see what God is trying to tell me. I think maybe it's coming in a little different way for Charlie, that God has given him an idea, an insight that allowed him to know what was the right way to go. With me, I get lots of different ideas. I try each one of them, and sometimes they work out. This is the way it is. People have different styles. I think God uses us in different ways according to our abilities, maybe just according to different ways that God sees that it will be useful for us to explore the universe. It's all very different.

TDS: One very interesting thing you said is that you are doing this because God wants you to do it in this way.

WDP: I think so. Yes, I think that exploring the universe is a holy calling, as are many other callings. I think that creating art, music and literature is also a holy calling, and I believe that exploring the universe is also a holy calling for a scientist. I think that God has given us the gifts to do that, and He has given each of us different gifts. Look at somebody like Einstein, he was given gifts so far beyond the gifts that most of us were given, and as a result he saw such things that I can't imagine how I would have been able to see. So that was a different kind of gift from the kind of gift that I've been given. I've been given a gift of skill in my hands to put together apparatus that will work. So, I think of myself as being much more of a workman in the kinds of things that I do than somebody like Einstein or Charlie Townes.

TDS: But one thing that I could say is that creativity, I think, has some kind of connection with the mental state of the individual. When a person is in a happy state of mind, he is prepared to receive the gift of creativity from God. I think that when one becomes angry or upset, then creative or useful ideas won't come.

God has given to each of us some skill and certain ability. There is an important passage in the Bhagavad-gita: *teṣāṁ satata-yuktānāṁ bhajatāṁ prīti-pūrvakam dadāmi buddhi-yogaṁ tam yena mām upayānti te;* meaning, to the degree that one

... exploring the universe is also a holy calling for a scientist.

— Phillips

... creativity has some kind of connection with the mental state of the individual. When a person is in a happy state of mind, he is prepared to receive the gift of creativity from God. I think that when one becomes angry or upset, then creative or useful ideas won't come.

— T. D. Singh

surrenders, the Lord gives the gift of knowledge so that one can have a personal devotional relationship with God.[8] Thus the gifts from God come to different individuals in different degrees.

WDP: Yes, that may be so. But you said another thing that I think is very important to me, about being in the company of other people and having a good experience. To me it seems that most of the good things that happen scientifically have happened in the company of others. I know there are scientists who say – and I'm sure that it is true – that they do their best work alone, and that's wonderful. I don't do my best work alone. I do my best work in the company of other people, people with whom I can share ideas. I can tell them my ideas and I can say, "Oh, well what about this," and they'll say, "Oh, well what about this." For me, that interplay of ideas is the way in which I make progress, but I know that's not true for everybody. For some people, the way they make progress is sitting alone and thinking and finally coming up with that great inspiration. It's wonderful that there are different ways in which inspiration comes. Maybe that's one of the reasons why I believe so strongly that relationships are so important, because it just seems that all good things that have happened to me have been a result of relationships.

TDS: One thing that I observed in my travel around the world and meeting different important people is that sometimes this openness or willingness to discuss has become much more visible after 9/11. Many scientists are interested in knowing why people are fighting each other in the name of religion and God. The scientists, especially, are becoming very open-minded today.

WDP: Well, I certainly agree that being open-minded is an important thing. I think that scientists try to be open to new ideas as part of their training. I'm certainly very happy that openness extends to ideas of faith, to ideas of other non-scientific areas. As scientists, I think that it is important for us to understand the significance of being open to new scientific ideas, and to extend that understanding of our openness to other kinds of ideas and to help other people in our society understand how important it is. Perhaps by telling stories about how important it is scientifically to be open-minded we can also make it more likely that people are open to other kinds of ideas as well.

TDS: Your involvement in the church is very important – it plays an important role in your life. Is it contributing anything to your scientific ideas?

WDP: Well, I would say it is indirectly helping me. Certainly my relationship to my church gives me a good platform for having a happy life. I really treasure the personal relationships that I have with the

> I think a better person can be a better scientist. ... the understanding I have about the way one ought to live - an understanding of what I believe God wants for us: this is something that carries over into the way I do my work, and I think it should be for every person of faith. Their faith, their religious moral principles, should be things that affect the way they do their work.
>
> — Phillips

people in my church. As you said, if you've got a happy life then it's more likely that you are going to have more creative power than what would otherwise be the case. Church adds to my personal well-being, and certainly helps me to be a better person, and I think a better person can be a better scientist. Also, the teaching of the church – the understanding I have about the way one ought to live - an understanding of what I believe God wants for us: this is something that carries over into the way I do my work, and I think it should be for every person of faith. Their faith, their religious moral principles, should be things that affect the way they do their work. You can't go to church on Sunday and say, "Well, we should love our neighbors as ourselves, we should love our enemies, we should be kind to everybody," and then on Monday morning go into work and do things that will undercut your colleagues, or write a paper in which you don't refer to their work so as to not give their work as much prominence as it might otherwise have got. You just shouldn't do those kinds of things. But I know that there are plenty of people who don't act in a kind way toward their colleagues. But for me, I have to act that way because that's part of the way I am. I'm not saying that I always act that way – nobody is perfect. We all have impulses that are less than what we wish they were, so I'm not always doing the right thing. But I always have that background. I'm grounded in my religious faith; my being part of the church helps to guide me to do the right thing.

> I'm grounded in my religious faith; my being part of the church helps to guide me to do the right thing.
>
> — Phillips

TDS: So when you are involved in the deep aspects of scientific research works, do your experiences in the church and in the power and mercy of the Lord help you to act the way that you do?

WDP: Well that's what I'm saying, that it helps me to be the kind of person that I think God wants me to be. Having that support from the church is an important part of my life. A lot of people would say, "Well, I can believe in God, I can worship God in my home, I don't need to go to church." But for me, going to church helps strengthen those ties. We talked about the personal relationship with God and the personal relationships with each other. For me, having those personal relationships with other people in church strengthens my personal relationship with God and gives me more of that personal inner strength that allows me to be the person that God wants me to be. It would be harder for me to be what God wants me to be if I didn't go to the church and did not have the support of other people.

TDS: I think that's a very wonderful thing. This culture of being dependent on the relationship with God is a wonderful thing. It is extremely inspiring to hear your own experience.

WDP: It is something that I treasure, but at the same time I have to admit that I don't always do what God wants me to do. We have a verse in our scriptures that says, "All have sinned and fallen short of the glory of God," and certainly I know that's true of myself. But I also know that God forgives me when I fall short and helps me to do better the next time.

TDS: It's very wonderful. "To err is human, to forgive is divine." You have wonderful qualities of humility and dependence on God. Now, I'm very new to the area of the laser cooling of atoms, but I'm very interested. Could you please explain a little bit about it to me?

WDP: The idea of laser cooling is that we have a gas of atoms or molecules. The air is one example; it is mostly molecules but there are some atoms. One of the characteristics of a gas is that the atoms and molecules that make up the gas are moving around very fast. What we do in laser cooling is to shine laser light onto a

gas of atoms and we make the atoms slow down in their motion. Making them slow down is the same as making the gas colder. If I say that I've got hot gas, it means that the atoms that make up that gas, or molecules that make up that gas, are moving faster than the same gas if it were cold. So slowing down the motion of the atoms in gas is the same as cooling. That's what we do in laser cooling. Now how do we do that? Well, we make the light push on the atoms. For a little more than a hundred years, people have known that light pushes on things and they suspected that it was true for even longer. For example, comet tails: since the time

THE CONCEPT BEHIND LASER COOLING OF ATOMS[9]

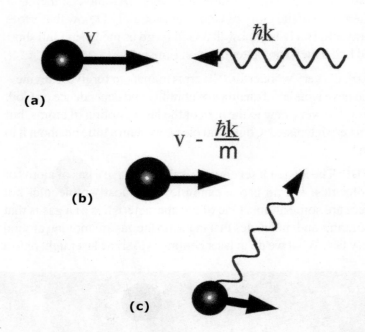

The basic process underlying the laser cooling of atoms is as follows: An atomic beam with a velocity 'v' is struck by an opposing laser beam, a stream of photons. For each photon that a ground-state atom absorbs, it is slowed by $v_{rec} = \hbar k/m$ ($k=2\pi/\lambda$ where λ is the wavelength of the light). In order to absorb again, the atom must return to the ground state by emitting a photon. Thus, after an extremely short time, normally around a hundred-millionth of a second, the retarded atom emits a photon. The emitted photon also has a momentum, which gives the atom a certain small recoil velocity. But the direction of the recoil varies at random, so that after many absorptions and emissions the speed of the atom has diminished considerably. If the absorption and emission are repeated many times, the mean velocity, and therefore the kinetic energy of the atom will be reduced. Since the temperature of an ensemble of atoms is a measure of the random internal kinetic energy, this is equivalent to cooling the atoms. This slowing down effect forms the basis for a powerful method of cooling atoms with laser light.

of Kepler, at least people have known that the tails of comets always point away from the sun. One of the reasons for that is that sunlight pushes on the dust and gas that make up the comet, creating the tail so it's always pointing away from the sun. There's also a solar wind that pushes, but the point is that light can push on

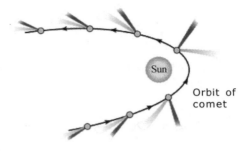

Comet and Sun: Tail of comet directed away from Sun. Gas (ion) tail (dark color) points straight away from Sun and dust tail (light color) curves towards orbital path. (Image Source: NASA)

things. So what we do is we arrange to have laser light push on atoms in such a way as to make them slow down. When they slow down, then the gas will be colder. That is, in a nutshell, how laser cooling works. We use the force that light can exert on atoms to push on them so as to make them slow down.

TDS: What are some of the future applications of this?

WDP: Well, we have been able to use laser-cooled atoms to make better clocks. This is one of the present applications. So today, the best clocks that we have are made with laser-cooled atoms, using the kinds of techniques that we have developed in this laboratory – and that other people in other laboratories have developed. (Certainly we weren't the only ones contributing to the development of laser cooling.) By using these techniques, people have been able to make the very best atomic clocks. What we mean by the 'second' is defined today by instruments that use laser-cooled atoms.

Time is a very important thing in our modern society. High-speed communications that are synchronous require that we have a very precise timing. Navigation using the Global Positioning System

(GPS) requires very precise timing. We will be expecting all these things to be improved in the future by making better clocks, and in particular, clocks that use laser-cooled atoms. So there's an example that's already happening today. Standards laboratories here in the U.S., and in the U.K., France, Germany, Japan, and elsewhere are all using laser cooling to make their time scales.

Vasudeva Rao (Henceforth **VR**): I was fascinated by your explanation of laser cooling in regards to calculating time using atomic clocks. Because in one of our ancient scriptures called the *Srimad Bhagavatam* (SB), which has been available in written form for more than 5,000 years, there is a chapter entitled "Calculation of Time from the Atom."[10] It is explained there that time is measured by the movement or vibration of the atoms. The similarity in concept is very striking. Can you please explain how you measure time with laser-cooled atoms?

WDP: In fact, that's exactly correct – it is based on what some people might call the vibration of the atoms. It's a conventional definition that we have come to as being the best way of defining time. Let me say what it is in more detail. As you probably know, atoms have energy levels, that is, they exist in certain discreet energy states and they cannot exist in states in between those energy states. For example, to take the explicit example that we use for defining time: one defines time according to the atomic vibrations, and I use the word "vibrations" loosely, of a cesium atom – vibrations of a particular kind. In a cesium atom you have a nucleus that is the center of the atom. The nucleus has a spin, and the spin has a magnetic moment so the nucleus behaves like a tiny magnet. There are also electrons that are outside the nucleus, and in the cesium atom there is one extra electron, which does most of the work in determining the chemical properties of the cesium atom, called the valence electron. So we have the nucleus here and all these electrons, and on the outside is the valence electron. The electron also has a spin and also has a magnetic moment, and the spin in the nucleus is in a particular direction.

स कालः परमाणुर्वै यो भुङ्क्ते परमाणुताम् ।
सतोऽविशेषभुग्यस्तु स कालः परमो महान् ॥

(Srimad Bhagavatam 3.11.4)

Calculation of Time from the Atom

Measuring time using 'vibrations' of atoms—this is the principle behind today's advanced atomic clocks. Surprisingly, the similar concept has been presented in the ancient vedantic text (*Srimad Bhagavatam*) which has been available in written form for more than 5,000 years. There is a complete chapter entitled "Calculation of Time from the Atom" in this miraculous literature.

The basic principle involved is very simple. The atomic orbits correspond to energy levels, and electrons can only move between energy levels when they absorb or release just the right amount of energy. This energy is absorbed or released in the form of electromagnetic radiation. It is the exact frequency of this electromagnetic radiation required to make the transition of electron between the two energy levels which determines the measure of time. Thus, today, the second is the duration of 9,192,631,770 periods of the radiation corresponding to the transition between the two hyperfine levels of the ground state of the cesium 133 atom.

These spins can be aligned in the same direction or they can be aligned in the opposite direction. Now it takes energy to go from one to the other. Because of the magnetic field between them, to turn the spin of the electron requires that you either put in energy or take it out. That energy can be put in or taken out by shining microwaves onto the atom. In order to make that transition from one spin state to the other, you have to shine microwaves that have a very specific frequency. It's that frequency that becomes the ticking of the atomic clock. That frequency is a very specific number, 9.18 and a whole bunch of other digits, billions of cycles per second, GHz. When you shine in exactly the right microwave frequency, you can make the cesium atom shift from one energy level to the other, and that frequency is what we use to keep time. We adjust our microwave frequency until it is just right to make that flip, and then you have a clock ticking at a certain nine and some giga-cycles per second, and that's our clock. But that was a choice that we made because it seemed like a good choice; it seemed like a very stable way of doing it. Before atomic clocks, we made other choices – the rotation of the Earth was the original definition for the second. We say the day is divided into a certain number of seconds – 24 hours x 60 minutes per hour x 60 seconds per minute. That comes to 86,400 seconds in a day – that was the definition of the second. But people figured out it wasn't a very good definition since the Earth is slowing down. It doesn't provide a completely stable definition of time. So people thought about other ways and eventually the atomic definition of time became, by international agreement, the way in which we define time. It might be that in the future we will come up with a different definition of time that is more precise and more capable of doing the things that we need to do, but for the moment this definition is working very well and we're using it to do all the things we need to do.

TDS: Thank you for explaining the mechanism of laser cooling of atoms and the working principles of atomic clock. I am sure it will have wide application in the near future. Time is also a very interesting concept in our Vedic tradition. It is regarded as the impersonal aspect of God. Within the current cosmological Big Bang model, time is understood differently than it is in our tradition. In the Big Bang model, time begins just after the Big Bang, whereas in the Vedic tradition time is eternal.

WDP: Yes, that's an interesting difference. I'm not sure if that is an important difference, but certainly it is something that we understand from the point of view of cosmology, that time doesn't have meaning before the Big Bang. But interestingly enough, early Christian scholars also said God created time when He created the universe. So that is an interesting idea. Now I don't believe that it's important for us as creatures of God to understand this in one way or another. For example, I don't believe I'll be a better person if I have a correct understanding of whether or not time began with the Big Bang, but I find it interesting that people have these different understandings, and in some cases ascribe religious significance to time.

TDS: And time and space – these two are connected.[12]

WDP: Certainly. It's one of the things that Einstein taught us, that time and space are interconnected, that we can't really separate time and space. I think that's a concept that we're still having a hard time understanding.

TDS: We were talking about the future of laser cooling of atoms. Can you tell me some of its other possible uses in day-to-day life?

WDP: Well, you know, day-to-day life is often hard to know about. But it's already a part of day-to-day life because, whether we realize it or not, we are affected by things like the Global Positioning System (GPS). If somebody delivers a package to you, he may use GPS to find your address. If you fly in an airplane, the pilots use the GPS to navigate that airplane. So atomic clocks are already being used in things that do affect your life. Laser-cooled atomic clocks are the best atomic clocks, and they're being used in the synchronization of the GPS. The atomic clocks are also used in satellites. There is a constellation of satellites each of which

Global Positioning System (GPS)

Originally developed by the US Department of Defense to provide all-weather round-the-clock navigation capabilities for military ground, sea, and air forces, GPS has also become an integral asset in numerous civilian applications and industries around the globe. GPS employs 24 spacecrafts in 20,200 km circular orbits inclined at 55 degrees. These spacecrafts are placed in 6 orbit planes with four operational satellites in each plane. Global Positioning System satellites transmit signals to equipment on the ground and the GPS receivers on ground convert the satellite's signals into position, velocity, and time estimates for navigation, positioning, time dissemination, or geodesy. GPS technology has made a huge impact on navigation and positioning needs and it has become possible to track aircrafts, cars, cell phones, boats and even individuals. Today, GPS is finding its way into cars, boats, planes, construction equipment, moviemaking gear, farm machinery, and even laptop computers.[11]

contains several atomic clocks. The satellites send information about the time, and with a GPS receiver you can receive these signals from several of these satellites and determine where you are anywhere on the surface of the earth. The atomic clocks in the satellites are not yet laser-cooled atomic clocks, but they are guided by a time system that uses laser-cooled atomic clocks. Maybe one day even the clocks that are in the satellites will be laser-cooled. I don't know. But in any case, I would say that good time is something that does affect our lives even though it may not be evident to us. Now, will this kind of technology ever affect our lives in a way that is more evident, the way, for example, the laser has affected our lives? Charlie Townes and his colleagues have invented the laser, and for a while some people said the laser is a solution in search of a problem. But today nobody would say that, mainly because most of us have multiple lasers in our houses. If you have a computer with a CD-ROM in it, there are lasers used in the reading and writing of the CD. When we make a telephone call, often the voice transmission or data communication is done by fiber optics, which use lasers to transmit information. So the invention of the laser has affected our daily lives in a way that is evident to people. You can see many instruments that are using lasers regularly. Lasers are in our houses. But I'm not sure if anybody is going to have laser-cooled things in their houses in the future.

TDS: You may never know.

WDP: Yes. You may never know, because I'm not sure that a few years ago anybody would have imagined that we would all have lasers in our houses. Or for that matter, a few years ago people wouldn't have imagined we would all have computers in our houses. Rather recently people who were the presidents of big computer companies made statements to the effect that there was no reason for anyone to have a computer in their home, and now, in the U.S., almost everyone has a computer – maybe several computers – in their home. There is also a whole bunch of computers that people don't even think of as being computers. A computer is in your microwave oven, a computer is in your washing machine, a computer is in your car. All these are computers that you may not even think about, in addition to the laptop or desktop computers that we have. So you're right, you never know. It might be that some of these things would turn out to be household items, but at the moment I can't see it.

TDS: Do you have any general suggestions for students and young scholars who want to have a career in science?

WDP: I guess if I had to give advice to young people who want to have a career in science, the thing that I would say is be curious. That's the most important thing. Of course, being curious in a certain sense is the same thing as seeking and being open to what you want to find, including all parts of what we've been talking about this afternoon. One should be conscious of this holy calling, of being open to what nature or God has to tell us as being something that we should aspire to; I think curiosity implies those features. Curiosity is one of the most important things that a scientist can have. I think all of us start off with a tremendous amount of curiosity as children. What you need to do, in order to be a successful scientist, is to maintain that childlike curiosity.

TDS: What you just said about being curious seems very similar

> ... be curious. ... One should be conscious of this holy calling, of being open to what nature or God has to tell us as being something that we should aspire to; I think curiosity implies those features. ... What you need to do, in order to be a successful scientist, is to maintain that childlike curiosity.
>
> — Phillips
>
> ... one must be curious to search about the nature of the absolute truth.
>
> — T. D. Singh

to our *Vedantic* tradition. *Veda* means knowledge, and *anta* means end. *Vedanta* is the Hindu concept of the ultimate knowledge and ultimate reality. The first aphorism of *Vedanta* says, in Sanskrit, *athāto brahma jijñāsā*. This means that one must be curious to search about the nature of the absolute truth.[13] It is very, very similar to what you said.

It seems that the present scientific method is not sufficient to study the nature of consciousness. Roger Penrose said that "in order to study consciousness we need a new science."[14] I was wondering whether you had any thoughts along that line.

WDP: Yes. Well, I guess we don't know. What Penrose says might be true. Consciousness is a phenomenon that is so far beyond our present understanding that it may very well be that we need a different approach in order to understand it. On the other hand, what we sometimes call the scientific method, I think, is an idea that is more beloved by philosophers than by scientists. I think that somebody said that the scientific method is to get the answer. Philosophers talk about what the scientific method is. It dates from the time of maybe Francis Bacon or Galileo. You do experiments to figure out what's going on. I don't think anyone could have imagined how far that scientific method would take us into the kinds of things that we know about the way the universe works today. We can compare what Galileo knew and what we know – there's an incredible difference. I'm not sure we'll be able to understand things like consciousness in detail using the kind of general methods that Galileo and others began with. So I'm not going to say that I believe that the present methods for scientific investigation are incapable of understanding things as complex as consciousness. But at the same time I'm not going to say that we now have the tools we require to understand consciousness, or even that we ever will completely understand it. That's also a logical possibility. Maybe we will never understand consciousness. There is a passage from our scripture that says now we are seeing in a mirror, dimly, but later, when we are in full union with God, we will see Him face to face. Right now our knowledge is imperfect, but later it will be perfect. It may mean there are some things we simply will not understand in the context of this earth and this universe, but maybe we will. I just don't know. When you have something so remote as consciousness from what we understand today, it's hard to tell whether you will eventually understand, and it's not beyond the realm of possibility that we will not understand it.

TDS: In our tradition consciousness is regarded as existing in the spiritual realm – just like in matter we have fundamental particles, similarly consciousness is a fundamental property of the spiritual realm. So in that sense, I agree with you that we may never be able to profit by our current scientific devices, which are in the material realm. But Penrose says we need a new science to understand consciousness. However, he does not spell out what the new science would look like.

WDP: Yes. People talk about a new science, although I haven't yet seen something that I would consider to be so different from today's science that I would call it a new science. Or, I should say there is nothing so different from traditional science that I would call it a new science. But I have a great deal of sympathy with your suggestion about consciousness being something that is in the spiritual realm. I have a guess – this is only a guess, certainly not a scientific conclusion – that consciousness itself is a gift from God. That is something that is given to us, to creatures, not something that is part of the material nature of those creatures, but is an external gift that has a spiritual content. And those creatures that are spiritual are creatures that have this consciousness, have self-awareness. Now whether that is only a quality of human beings, I'm not entirely sure. But certainly, it's something that is characteristic of living creatures and is not characteristic of non-living creatures. I don't know if it is characteristic of all living creatures. For example, I don't know if single-celled animals have consciousness. It seems unlikely that

In our (Vedantic) tradition consciousness is regarded as existing in the spiritual realm – just like in matter we have fundamental particles, similarly consciousness is a fundamental property of the spiritual realm.

— T. D. Singh

I have a guess – this is only a guess, certainly not a scientific conclusion – that consciousness itself is a gift from God. That is something that is given to us, to creatures, not something that is part of the material nature of those creatures, but is an external gift that has a spiritual content. And those creatures that are spiritual are creatures that have this consciousness, have self-awareness. Now whether that is only a quality of human beings, I'm not entirely sure. But certainly, it's something that is characteristic of living creatures and is not characteristic of non-living creatures.

— Phillips

single-celled animals have consciousness of the sort that we have been talking about. We haven't really defined what consciousness is, and of course it's difficult to define what we mean by consciousness.

TDS: According to our scriptures all living forms have consciousness. Even single-celled animals have consciousness, but on a very, very low level.[15] According to *Vedanta,* consciousness evolves from the lower form of life to the higher form. In the science and religion dialogue, discussion about consciousness often comes up. In the USA there has been much debate about evolution and when and how consciousness arises. It deeply involves both the scientific and religious principles. Do you have any comment about evolution?

WDP: To me it seems that the scientific evidence in favor of an evolutionary description – not just the development of species but also the development of the universe itself – is so strongly supported by scientific evidence that there seems to be no question that this is the way in which the things were done. What I believe is that these are tools that God used to bring about the sort of things that were inherent in creation from the beginning. What I believe is that God gave to creation the potential to be the kind of universe that we have now, and that evolution was one of the ways in which that potential was realized as being part of what God wanted. For me, I don't see any conflict with my conception of God as the loving Creator who wanted to have relationships with living, conscious creatures and the mechanism of His creation.

TDS: In *Sanskrit* the soul is called *atman.* Its symptom is consciousness and it is synonymous with life. Consciousness is the spiritual quality of life and is nonphysical and eternally existing. Unless the soul is within the body, unless life is within the body, the body will not develop. So we place priority on life and emphasize the transmigration of the soul, or evolution of consciousness. In the *Vedas* this understanding is given. I think it might be useful to have a deeper dialogue amongst different traditions so that we

... we are divinely created beings; we have souls and we have responsibilities. Research won't change the fundamental truth that we have souls and that those souls connect with the divine.

— Phillips

can come to a reasonable understanding of the soul, life, or consciousness and its nature.

WDP: It certainly is an area that is going to require a great deal more study if we are going to have any understanding. As we were discussing, it may be that we will always lack complete understanding. But, at least for me, we are divinely created beings; we have souls and we have responsibilities. Research won't change the fundamental truth that we have souls and that those souls connect with the divine.

Abhishek Tiwari (Henceforth **AT**): I wanted to bring up the topic of students again. I am a graduate student and I see two different groups of students in my school: there are students who are not very serious about God, and there are students who have a very strong conception of God because of their upbringing, like you. But they are shy to speak about it; they are not very open about it.

WDP: Okay, so how should it be? You know, this is always a problem for people. To use a word that is common in Christianity, how could you "witness" to your faith? This is the word we often use in the Christian tradition, how do you witness to your faith? What that means is how you display the fact that you are a person of faith so as to benefit somebody else. I'm afraid that the answer is different for every person because different people have different skills. Some people like to preach. They say, "this is what I believe and here are the reasons why I believe it and I'll let you consider if you believe the same thing." Other people take a more, shall we say, subtle approach that we sing about in a hymn in our church called, "Faith of Our Fathers." Do you know what I mean?

TDS: Yes, I do.

WDP: (Sings) "Faith of our fathers, holy faith." Anyway, there's a line in it that says, "And preach thee, too, as love knows how, by kindly words and virtuous life." So for some of us, the way in which we witness to our faith is by being kind to others and living a virtuous life, and people understand that we do that because of our faith. That will have an effect on others. So if people know you are a person of faith, and you're also a nice guy; you don't do things that are nasty to other people; you help other people whenever you can, then they'll think there is some connection – he is a person of faith. They are going to notice any person who is kind and good to other people. Each person, I think, must come to understand how they are led by the spirit to witness, to demonstrate their faith. Some people may be led by the spirit to witness by the very state of their lives. Other people will be led to be more direct, to actually try to convince people through discussion and discourse. You have to understand what your skills are. God has not given us all the same skills. We are not all meant to be preachers. So you have to decide.

> God is wonderful, and when I look at results of science, it just increases my wonder at how great God is.
>
> — Phillips

AT: Another thing I am wondering about is, do you think science will take on a more theistic aspect? Right now there is a perception that science is atheistic.

WDP: I don't agree with that. I don't believe that science is either atheistic or theistic. Science is science. There are theistic people who do science and there are atheistic people who do science, and I think that the theistic people who do science have more fun.

VR: So here is a problem. Some people want to have faith in the writings of their respective scriptures but they also want to believe in what they can scientifically observe or theorize. Do you feel there is a way for a person to integrate these two aspects in their life?

WDP: Yes. I have no problem with integrating it. God is wonderful, and when I look at results of science, it just increases my wonder at how great God is.

TDS: I have one last question. It is about how to bring peace and harmony in society so we will be free from terrorism and man-made disturbances. There are a lot of peace summits and, of course, there is the work of the United Nations, but there doesn't seem to be much progress in achieving real peace. It seems to me that if the two disciplines of science and spirituality, or science and religion were to work in a cooperative way, then I think there could be some important groundwork for achieving lasting peace, since scientists provide the intellectual background for making bombs and weaponry and the fanatic religious groups seem to be at the root of many conflicts. It would be very beneficial if the scientists and religious groups come together and discuss how to live peacefully by engaging in a very serious dialogue on how to use their respective fields of knowledge for the betterment of the whole human family. I would appreciate your comments in this regard.

WDP: It is certainly very disturbing to me that there are instances in the world where the lack of peace seems to have been motivated by religious conflict. This is so disappointing to me because it seems that all the people who are involved in these religious conflicts are affirming a belief in God, who wants peace and who constantly has told us that peace is good. Yet the conflict is perpetrated and perpetuated by people who believe in a God of peace and love. So I find the case so disheartening. But the thing that you're suggesting, that somehow a combination of scientific thinking and religious thinking may be the way of finally breaking through this barrier and finally getting to this ultimate peace – I find that to be a very appealing idea because, on the one hand, you have people who are dogmatic about their religion, who are not open to other kinds of thinking. Science by its nature must be open to other kinds of thinking. But, of course, we know there are some scientists who aren't open to religious thinking. If somehow we can bring together the idea of openness present in science with religious thinking that has ideas of love and peace at its base, maybe that is the way. But we've been trying for a long time. For thousands of years we've been suffering from wars and conflict, and I certainly hope that this is going to change. But if I had to predict, it's hard to see that these conflicts are going to be easily resolved. People need to have love in their hearts for these things to change. When people have love in their hearts, then things will change.

TDS: All the scriptures proclaim that we are all God's children. Hence we are all brothers and sisters although we speak different

... if the two disciplines of science and spirituality, or science and religion were to work in a cooperative way, then I think there could be some important groundwork for achieving lasting peace, since scientists provide the intellectual background for making bombs and weaponry and the fanatic religious groups seem to be at the root of many conflicts. It would be very beneficial if the scientists and religious groups come together and discuss how to live peacefully by engaging in a very serious dialogue on how to use their respective fields of knowledge for the betterment of the whole human family.

— T. D. Singh

If somehow we can bring together the idea of openness present in science with religious thinking that has ideas of love and peace at its base, maybe that is the way. ... When people have love in their hearts, then things will change.

— Phillips

languages, have different colors and different religions. If we recognize and practice this culture of universal brotherhood and sisterhood because we have one common father, then the world will be a very different place.

WDP: Yes, I think so. Certainly for me, everything that I do is made easier because of my faith in God, and I certainly think that it will be easier to solve the big problems that face this world if we rely on that faith.

TDS: Well, we covered a wide range of topics.

WDP: Yes, indeed.

> All the scriptures proclaim that we are all God's children. Hence we are all brothers and sisters although we speak different languages, have different colors and different religions. If we recognize and practice this culture of universal brotherhood and sisterhood because we have one common father, then the world will be a very different place.
>
> — T. D. Singh

TDS: I would really like to thank you for your time.

WDP: You're most welcome. I'm glad you were interested in coming to have this discussion, and I wish you all well in your efforts.

TDS: Have you been to India before?

WDP: I have not been to India. This is one of the great gaps in my education as a human being. I have not been to India, but it is certainly one of the things that I look forward to.

TDS: I'm organizing an international conference as part of the opening celebrations of a University I am constructing. The focus is on science and spirituality and world peace. It is scheduled for 2007. I have organized many conferences with different themes centered on science and spirituality.

WDP: Well, please send me some information about the

conference and I'll see if it's possible to participate.

TDS We are planning to publish a new book on science and spirituality. One of my assistants is working on that and he asked me to ask you if we could publish the paper you wrote in connection with Science and the Spiritual Quest.

WDP: The paper that was written for Science and the Spiritual Quest was based on a presentation in Cambridge, Massachusetts. I also did a presentation in Paris, but there wasn't a paper that resulted from that. They did have a meeting in Paris a month or so ago, and in connection with that, I think they reprinted the paper that I wrote for the Cambridge meeting. I think that they translated it and reprinted it. They had asked me if they could reprint it.

TDS: Do we have your permission to reprint it?

WDP: Yes, I'm certainly happy to have you reprint it. I think it is called *Ordinary Faith, Ordinary Science*. I certainly grant my permission to reprint that.

TDS: Thank you Prof. Phillips. I just want to express that I met several scholars around the world in different communities but my meeting with you is something very special which I will greatly treasure. I feel this must be the Lord's arrangement.

WDP: It's been a blessing.

> Certainly for me, everything that I do is made easier because of my faith in God, and I certainly think that it will be easier to solve the big problems that face this world if we rely on that faith.
>
> — Phillips

Notes and References

1. *Science, Spirituality and the Nature of Reality*, A discussion between Sir Roger Penrose and Dr. T. D. Singh, Kolkata, 2005.

2. "Amazing Light: Visions for Discovery," An International Symposium in honor of the 90th Birthday Year of Charles Townes, Oct. 6-8, 2005, University of California, Berkeley. Web: www.foundationalquestions.net/townes

3. Proceedings of the conference was published by the Bhaktivedanta Institute as *Thoughts on Synthesis of Science and Religion*, eds. T. D. Singh and Samaresh Bandyopadhyay, Calcutta, 2001.

4. Refer www.metanexus.net

5. A.C. Bhaktivedanta Swami Śrīla Prabhupāda, *Śrīmadbhāgavatam*, Canto 1, Ch. 2 Verse 11, Bhaktivedanta Book Trust, Bombay, 1987, p.103.

6. A.C. Bhaktivedanta Swami Śrīla Prabhupāda, *Śrīmadbhāgavatam*, Canto 3, Ch. 26 Verse 49, Bhaktivedanta Book Trust, Bombay, 1987.

7. Refer *Savijñānam – Scientific Exploration for a Spiritual Paradigm*, Kolkata, 2003, vol.2, pp. 5-6 & table of constants on p. 79.

8. A. C. Bhaktivedanta Swami Prabhupada, *Bhagavad Gita As It Is*, Chapter 10, verse 10.

9. Refer for more details William Phillips Nobel Lecture, "Laser Cooling and Trapping of Neutral Atoms," Dec 8, 1997.

10. A. C. Bhaktivedanta Swami Prabhupada, *Śrīmadbhāgavatam*, Canto 3, Part 1, Los Angeles Bhaktivedanta Book Trust, pp. 459-490.

11. *Merriam-Webster's Collegiate Encyclopedia*, Massachusetts, USA, 2000, p. 660.

12. Einstein gave a completely new model for space and time in his special theory of relativity in the year 1905. His theory is based on two important axioms:

(a) The laws of science should be the same for all freely moving observers (observers in different inertial frames of reference).

(b) The speed of light through vacuum is the same for all observers in inertial frames of reference. This was experimentally shown by Michelson and Morley.

From these axioms Einstein showed that the time interval and the space interval between two events measured in one inertial (freely moving, non-accelerating) frame of reference would not be the same in another inertial frame of reference.

Using the two axioms, Einstein also showed that the space-time interval between two events which is defined as:

$$(\Delta S)^2 - c^2(\Delta t)^2 = (\Delta x)^2 + (\Delta y)^2 + (\Delta z)^2 + (ic\Delta t)^2$$

(where $i = \sqrt{-1}$) is the same for all inertial frame of reference and Δx, Δy, Δz and $ic\Delta t$ are treated as components of a single vector (space-time vector). For more details, refer *Savijñānam – Scientific Exploration for a Spiritual Paradigm*, Journal of the Bhaktivedanta Institute, Kolkata, 2003, vol.2, pp. 70-75. Also refer Stephen Hawking, *A Brief History of Time*, 1996, Tenth anniversary edition, USA, pp. 20-21.

13. Refer T. D. Singh's article on this verse: "Vedanta and Science-I: Human Life and Evolution of Consciousness," *Savijñānam – Scientific Exploration for a Spiritual Paradigm*, Journal of the Bhaktivedanta Institute, Vol.1, Kolkata, 2002, pp. 51-74.

14. *Science, Spirituality and the Nature of Reality*, A discussion between Sir Roger Penrose and Dr. T. D. Singh, Kolkata, 2005.

15. A fabulous description of microbes' communication and intelligence is given by Mark Buchanan, *New Scientist,* London, Nov 20-Nov 26, 2004, Vol. 184, Iss. 2474, pp. 34-37. The well-known biologist, George Wald and others such as, Lynn Marguilis also indicated that Protozoa, single-celled animals and bacteria possess consciousness. Refer: Eds. L. Margulis, J. O. Corlis, M. Melkonian and D. J. Chapman, *Handbook of Protoctista: The structure, cultivation, habitats and life histories of eukaryotic microorganisms and descendants exclusive of animals, plant and fungi.* Jones & Bartlett, Boston, 1990, p. 914.

About the Editor

Dr. T. D. Singh (His Holiness Bhaktisvarupa Damodara Swami) (1937-): A scientist and spiritualist known for his pioneering efforts to interface between science and religion for a deeper understanding of life and the universe, he received his Ph. D. in Physical Organic Chemistry from the University of California, Irvine in 1974. He has contributed many papers in the *Journal of American Chemical Society* and *the Journal of Organic Chemistry* in the field of fast proton transfer kinetics in model biological systems using stopped-flow technique and NMR spectroscopy. He also worked on gas phase reaction mechanisms using Ion Cyclotron Resonance (ICR) spectroscopy. He underwent Vaishnava Vedanta Studies (1970-77) under His Divine Grace Srila Prabhupada and he was appointed by Srila

Prabhupada as Director of the Bhaktivedanta Institute (1974-), which is a center to promote studies about the relationship between science and Vedanta. He has organized four International conferences on science and religion—First and Second World Congress for the Synthesis of Science and religion (Bombay, 1986 & Calcutta, 1997), First International Conference on the Study of Consciousness within Science (San Francisco, 1990) and Second International Congress on Life and Its Origin - Exploration from Science and Spiritual Traditions (Rome, 2004), where a galaxy of prominent scientists and religious leaders including several Nobel Laureates participated. He has authored and edited several books including *What is Matter and What is Life?* (1977), *Theobiology* (1979), *Vedanta & Science Series: Life and Origin of the Universe* (2004), *Life and Spiritual Evolution* (2005), and *Essays on Science and Religion* (2005), *(Ed.) Synthesis of Science and Religion: Critical Essays and Dialogues* (1987), *Thoughts on Synthesis of Science and Religion* (2001), *Seven Nobel Laureates on Science and Spirituality* (2004), *Science, Spirituality and the Nature of Reality* (2005), and *Towards a Culture of Harmony and Peace* (2005). He is the Editor-in-Chief of the Journal of the Bhaktivedanta Institute entitled, *Savijnanam: Scientific Exploration for a Spiritual Paradigm.*

Dr. Singh is also the President of Vedanta and Science Educational Research Foundation, Kolkata and a founding member of the United Religions Initiative (URI). He is president of URI's Manipur (North-Eastern India) Cooperation Circle. As an educator, he has established a network of schools in North-Eastern India and supervises and guides over 4000 students at these different schools. He is also an accomplished singer, instrumentalist, and poet. He founded "Ranganiketan Manipuri Cultural Arts Troupe" which has approximately 600 performances at over 300 venues in about 20 countries. He is building the University of Bhagavata Culture in Imphal, Manipur, India which will promote the universal scientific and philosophical relevance of the teachings of *Bhagavadgita, Srimad Bhagavatam,* Vedanta and other Vedic literatures within the framework of modern cultural and educational milieu for the welfare of humanity.

THE BHAKTIVEDANTA INSTITUTE

The Bhaktivedanta Institute was founded by His Divine Grace A. C. Bhaktivedānta Swami Prabhupāda in Vrindavan in August 1974. Śrīla Prabhupāda was one of the greatest exponents of Vedic culture in the 20th Century. He strongly felt that modern civilization is completely misdirected by scientific materialism and there is an urgent need to introduce the spiritual knowledge and wisdom of the *Bhagavad-gītā* and *Śrīmad-bhāgavatam*, the cream of all the Vedic literatures, to the scientists, philosophers, scholars and students of the world. He noticed that all the prestigious academic institutions and universities of the world were teaching many different subjects but they had left out the most important branch of knowledge— the science of the soul. He envisioned that this spiritual knowledge of life would help restore an ethical culture for modern society. Thus, there would be hope for bringing lasting happiness and world peace. He felt that introducing this spiritual culture should be the contribution of India for the welfare of humanity. Śrīla Prabhupāda appointed his disciple Dr. T. D. Singh (Bhaktisvarūpa Dāmodara Swami) as the director of the Institute from its very inception and left several instructions to him to carry forward his vision.

The Bhaktivedanta Institute is a center for Advanced Studies in Science and Vedānta and focuses on a consciousness-based paradigm. This spiritual paradigm has a unique potential to resolve the mind-body problem, the question of evolution and life's origin and many other philosophical and ethical concerns. Thus this paradigm will have profound significance for science, religion, and their synthesis. One of the primary objectives of the Bhaktivedanta Institute is to present this paradigm for the critical attention of serious scholars and thinkers throughout the world. As such, the institute supports a closer examination of existing scientific paradigms in cosmology, evolution, physics, biology, and other sciences. The institute also promotes scientific, philosophical and religious dialogues among scientists, scholars and theologians of the world covering various common conceptual grounds of science and religion for the purpose of creating a better and harmonious understanding among all people. In order to achieve these goals the institute organizes international conferences regularly and publishes books and journals. Interested persons may contact the secretary of the Institute at:

The Bhaktivedanta Institute
RC-8, Raghunathpur,
Manasi Manjil Building, Fourth Floor
VIP Road, Kolkata 700 059, India
Tel/Fax: +91-33-2500-9018; Tel: +91-33-2500-6091
E-mail: info@binstitute.org
Website: www.binstitute.org

BHAKTIVEDANTA INSTITUTE'S
RECENT PUBLICATIONS

THOUGHTS ON SYNTHESIS OF SCIENCE AND RELIGION

Editors: T. D. Singh & S. Bandyopadhyay
pp.735, Hardbound; 16 Color plates
US$25/Rs.1150
ISBN: 81-901369-0-9

This major publication by the Bhaktivedanta Institute contains learned articles on the synthesis of science and religion from **42 eminent scholars, religious leaders and scientists of the world including five Nobel Laureates**. The volume was formally released as a part of annual **Indian Science Congress** and is highly appreciated by the **President of India Dr. A. P. J. Abdul Kalam**. Containing 7 main sections, the volume reflects some possible grounds for the synthesis of science and religion and covers a wide variety of subject matters including faith, ethics, culture, consciousness, biology, quantum mechanics, Ecology/Environment, Biomedical Ethics for the 21st Century, and World Peace. It further explores the exciting and evocative work emerging in the fields of neuroscience, artificial intelligence, cognitive science, psychology, philosophy and a vast body of spiritual and religious experiences.

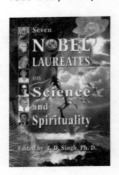

SEVEN NOBEL LAUREATES ON SCIENCE AND SPIRITUALITY

Editor: Dr. T. D. Singh
pp.112, Softbound
Rs.125/US$15; ISBN: 81-901369-2-5

This unique book edited by Dr. T. D. Singh consists of two dialogues and five essays. This is a sincere effort to bring so many Nobel Laureates together in one publication discussing Science and Spirituality. These seven great contributors are: (1) Prof. Charles Townes, *Nobel Laureate in Physics* (2) Prof. Werner Arber, *Nobel Laureate in Physiology and Medicine* (3) His Holiness The Dalai Lama, *Nobel Laureate in Peace* (4) Prof. George Wald, *Nobel Laureate in Physiology and Medicine* (5) Ms. Betty Williams, *Nobel Laureate in Peace* (6) Prof. B. D. Josephson, *Nobel Laureate in Physics* (7) Prof. Richard R. Ernst, *Nobel Laureate in Chemistry*.

These contemporary thinkers explore the link between science and spirituality in several areas of human concern such as, the role of Science and Religion in the search for the Origin of Life, the study of the nature of Consciousness, understanding the purpose behind the Universe, the role of Faith and Ethical Challenges. These dialogues and essays were earlier published under different titles by the Bhaktivedanta Institute. With an Introduction by Dr. T. D. Singh and the invaluable insights of the great thinkers presented in this volume, the book is an invaluable resource for all interested in the emerging field of science and spirituality.

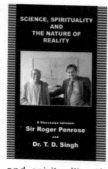

SCIENCE, SPIRITUALITY AND THE NATURE OF REALITY

A Dialogue between Dr. T. D. Singh and Sir Roger Penrose
pp.112, Softbound
Rs.95/US$3; ISBN: 81-901369-7-6

Since antiquity, many prominent thinkers of the world, from Plato to Tagore and from Newton to Einstein, have attempted to unveil the nature of reality. But reality seems always deeper than our feeble minds can comprehend. Can a combined effort of science and spirituality, the two most dominant forces of humanity, help to delve deeper into the nature of reality? This unique dialogue between Dr. T. D. Singh and Sir Roger Penrose; like the well-known East-West dialogue between Tagore and Einstein, is a sincere attempt to seek some possible answers to the question of reality. Reflecting on a wide range of topics from consciousness to cosmology and from scientific mystery to mathematical beauty, this dialogue will provide readers with useful insights in their quest for the ultimate reality.

LIFE AND SPIRITUAL EVOLUTION

Dr. T. D. Singh (His Holiness Bhaktisvarupa Damodara Swami)
pp.48, Softbound
Rs.65/US$1.5; ISBN: 81-901369-6-8

Today, the concept of evolution has influenced the whole world. It is taught in almost all schools and colleges of the world and is influencing thousands of students around the globe every moment. Life, according to this paradigm, is a product of the evolution of the lifeless cosmic dust particles (atoms and molecules), which have no meaning and purpose. However, all religious traditions of the world proclaim a divine meaning and higher purpose of life. Vedanta, the topmost philosophical treatise of spiritual and cultural heritage of India, provides a vivid description about life, its origin and meaning. Taking insights from the Vedantic literatures, the author, Dr. T. D. Singh, presents in this book a new holistic paradigm about life incorporating the spiritual dimension of life and evolution of consciousness. This Vedantic paradigm has the potential to look deeper into the nature of life.

113

VEDANTA AND SCIENCE SERIES: LIFE AND ORIGIN OF THE UNIVERSE

His Holiness Bhaktisvarupa Damodara
Swami (Dr. T. D. Singh)
pp.84, Softbound
Rs.75/US$2; ISBN: 81-901369-3-3

Since the dawn of civilization, all philosophical, scientific, religious and even artistic works, in principle, have centered around the study of life, its meaning and the origin of the universe. What is life? What is the origin of the universe? Is there any meaning and purpose behind the manifestation of life and the universe? What is the unseen cause behind the manifestation of the perceivable universe? These questions have puzzled all the great thinkers around the world over the ages. Vedanta, the topmost scientific and philosophical treatise of Indian spiritual and cultural heritage has a lot to contribute in this area and could provide a vital leap in expanding our knowledge of life and the origin of the universe. In this unique book, His Holiness Bhaktisvarupa Damodara Swami (Dr. T. D. Singh) investigates life and the secrets of the origin of the universe and depicts the relevance of Vedantic wisdom in the context of modern scientific and technological developments.

ESSAYS ON SCIENCE AND RELIGION

Dr. T. D. Singh (His Holiness Bhaktisvarupa
Damodara Swami)
pp.104, Softbound
Rs.85/US$2; ISBN: 81-901369-8-4

Science and religion are the two most dominant forces of humanity in the search for the ultimate meaning of life and the universe. Are these two forces reconcilable? If yes, what are the possible grounds for their synthesis? Could the recent developments in science and technology about human nature and the cosmos enable us to explore religious wisdom in new ways? In the pivotal times like ours, what role could science and religion dialogue play in restoring world peace? Moreover, what implications would this dialogue have on our future scientific researches? Reflecting on some of these profound issues, Dr. T. D. Singh (His Holiness Bhaktisvarupa Damodara Swami) presents in this volume four groundbreaking essays on science and religion. These four remarkable essays by him provide useful insights about the relationship between science and religion in our continuing quest for the deeper understanding of life and the universe.

GOD, INTELLIGENT DESIGN AND FINE-TUNING

A Dialogue between Dr. T. D. Singh and Prof. Michael J. Behe
pp.68, Softbound
Rs.95/US$ 3; ISBN: 81-89635-01-8

Is God no longer necessary in a world that is increasingly influenced by a scientific temper? Or, on the contrary, have the findings of modern sciences forced us to approach the question of the existence of God in new ways?

God, Intelligent Design and Fine-Tuning is a profound exchange between Dr. T. D. Singh and prominent biochemist Prof. Michael J. Behe from Lehigh University, Pennsylvania, USA, exploring how recent advancements in science points amazingly towards God. Over the past four decades modern biochemistry has uncovered the secrets of cells and has revealed us the marvelous design even at the molecular level. Advancements in science have also shown us some of the precise laws and unique fundamental constants in the universe. All these facts and observations point to a fine-tuned and specially designed universe with a purpose by a Supreme Being or God. As one journey through the newly discovered marvels of the cosmos and life discussed in this volume, one will be compelled to reexamine his opinion concerning the origins, evolution and essence of this wonderful world in which we live.

LIFE, MATTER AND THEIR INTERACTIONS

Dr. T. D. Singh (His Holiness Bhaktisvarupa Damodara Swami)
pp.124, Softbound
ISBN: 81-901369-9-2

The rapid advancements in science and technology have enabled us to penetrate deeper into the subatomic world and unfold many secrets behind various life processes. But are we now in a position to answer the question, 'what is life?' Is life an outcome of evolution of matter or a fundamentally different entity altogether? How do we explain various phenomena of life such as consciousness, free will, love, purpose, beauty, etc., which seem to be beyond the mere interaction of biomolecules? On the other hand, if life is beyond matter, how does it interact with matter and what laws does it follow? In this unique volume, the author, Dr. T. D. Singh, examines very closely the finer characteristics of life, matter and the nature of their interactions. The known physical laws of the present day, he proposes, seem quite insufficient to account for the features of life. Drawing insights from the ancient Vedantic texts, he thus presents an alternative view of life beyond molecules. Sixty years after Schrödinger's *What is life?*, this volume is a brilliant resource for all those interested to delve deeper into the deeper understanding of life.

TOWARDS A CULTURE OF HARMONY AND PEACE

pp.324 (16 Color Plates)
Hardbound (Rs.1125/US$25); Softbound (Rs.660/US$15); ISBN: 81-901369-4-1

Editor
Dr. T. D. Singh
Director, Bhaktivedanta Institute

Foreword
Desmond M. Tutu
Nobel Laureate in Peace

Dr. A. P. J. Abdul Kalam
President of India

H. H. The Dalai Lama
Nobel Laureate in Peace

Ms. Mairead Maguire
Nobel Laureate in Peace

Dr. Oscar Arias
Nobel Laureate in Peace

Mr. Adolfo Esquivel
Nobel Laureate in Peace

Dr. Manmohan Singh
Prime Minister of India

Prof. Ahmed Zewail
Nobel Laureate in Chemistry

Ms. Shirin Ebadi
Nobel Laureate in Peace

Prof. John Polanyi
Nobel Laureate in Chemistry

Prof. Jerome Karle
Nobel Laureate in Chemistry

Today, humanity is at a crossroads. We all feel tremendous anxiety, fear and unrest from terrorism and wars of various kinds. Thus every thinking person intensely yearns for harmony and peace in every corner of the globe. What are the ways and means for creating harmony and peace in this world where we have people with different cultures, religions, colors, nationalities, ideals, etc.? Could various religious traditions of the world guide humanity towards harmony and peace instead of being the cause of conflicts as seen in the past? Could interfaith dialogue provide some help at this critical juncture of humanity? Could the two most dominant forces of humanity in the quest of ultimate reality – science and spirituality be integrated to lead us to a peaceful world?

Reflecting on some of these issues, the Bhaktivedanta Institute and the Delhi Peace Summit brings together in this volume the wisdom from some of the most prominent thinkers of the world including Dr. A. P. J. Abdul Kalam, the President of India; Dr. Manmohan Singh, the Prime Minister of India; six Nobel Laureates in Peace and three Nobel Laureates in Science. This volume, containing 42 contributors, will provide all the readers useful insights and practical actions towards a culture of harmony and peace. To procure a copy of this volume, please send write to the Bhaktivedanta Institute, Kolkata.

ORDER FORM

SAVIJÑĀNAM

(You can also order online at
www.binstitute.org)

Scientific Exploration for a Spiritual Paradigm
Journal of the Bhaktivedanta Institute
(ISSN: 0972 - 6586)

Subscription Rates (one issue per year): India/Rest of the World

	2 issues		3 issues		4 issues	
	Rs.	US$	Rs.	US$	Rs.	US$
Individuals:	90	14	130	20	170	26
Institutions:	100	16	140	22	180	30
Students*:	80	12	115	18	150	24
Postage:	25	4	40	6	50	8

Please fill in block letters:

Name: ....

Address: ....

.... Zip:....................

Tel: .... Fax: .... email: ....

Subscription: ☐ Individual ☐ Institution ☐ Student   Date: ....

☐ Demand Draft/Cheque** enclosed (Payable to 'Bhaktivedanta Institute') for

Rs/US$ .... No.: .... Dated:................... Bank:....................

☐ Cash   *Please provide a xerox copy of valid student ID / ** Please add
Rs. 50 as bank clearing charges for outstation cheques*

Individual Copies of the Journal

Vol. 1

Vol. 2

Vol. 3&4
(combined)

The cost of individual volumes are:
Vol.1: Rs 80/US$8; **Vol.2**: Rs 100/US$9;
Vol.3&4 (combined): Rs 160/US$15
Postage and handling (per copy): Rs 10/US$2

Please send me the following volumes of the journal
*Savijnanam-Scientific Exploration for a Spiritual
Paradigm:* ☐ **Vol.1**   ☐ **Vol.2**   ☐ **Vol.3&4**

Name: ....

Address: ....

....

Tel: .... Fax: .... email: ....

Demand Draft/Cheque* enclosed (Payable to
'Bhaktivedanta Institute') for Rs/US$ ....
No.: .... Dated:................ Sign.:...................
*Please add Rs. 50 as bank clearing charges
for outstation cheques*

ORDER FORM

Please send me the following publications:

	Tick	No. of Copies
1. THOUGHTS ON SYNTHESIS OF SCIENCE AND RELIGION	☐	☐
2. SEVEN NOBEL LAUREATES ON SCIENCE AND SPIRITUALITY	☐	☐
3. SCIENCE, SPIRITUALITY AND THE NATURE OF REALITY	☐	☐
4. LIFE AND SPIRITUAL EVOLUTION	☐	☐
5. LIFE AND ORIGIN OF THE UNIVERSE	☐	☐
6. ESSAYS ON SCIENCE AND RELIGION	☐	☐
7. GOD, INTELLIGENT DESIGN AND FINE-TUNING	☐	☐
8. LIFE, MATTER AND THEIR INTERACTIONS	☐	☐
9. TOWARDS A CULTURE OF HARMONY AND PEACE	☐	☐
☐ Harbound ☐ Softbound		

Postage and handling (India/outside India):

For book no. 1 or 9: Rs 45/US$5 per book; Add Rs 25/US$3 for each additional copy

Others: Rs 10/US$2 per book; Add Rs 5/US$1 for each additional book

Please indicate whether books are for : ☐ Individual   ☐ Institution

Name: ....

Address: ....

....

Tel: .... Fax: .... email: ....

Demand Draft/Cheque* enclosed (Payable to 'Bhaktivedanta Institute') for Rs/US$ .... No.: .... Dated:................

Sign.:..................

Please add Rs. 50 as bank clearing charges for outstation cheques.

Also buy online at: www.binstitute.org

✉ Please mail the duly filled form to:

- ✂ - - -

THE BHAKTIVEDANTA INSTITUTE
RC-8, Raghunathpur,
Manasi Manjil Building, Fourth Floor
VIP Road, Kolkata 700 059, India
Tel/Fax: +91-33-2500-9018; Tel: +91-33-2500-6091